940.3
SHO

Shortal, John F.,
1951-

Forged by fire

$24.95

| DATE | | | |
|---|---|---|---|
| | | | |
| | | | |
| | | | |
| | | | |
| | | | |
| | | | |
| | | | |
| | | | |
| | | | |
| | | | |
| | | | |
| | | | |
| | | | |

# Forged by Fire

AMERICAN MILITARY HISTORY
Thomas L. Connelly, Editor


*Travels to Hallowed Ground*
by Emory M. Thomas

*Forged by Fire: General Robert L. Eichelberger
and the Pacific War*
by John F. Shortal

# FORGED BY FIRE

## General Robert L. Eichelberger and the Pacific War

by John F. Shortal

University of South Carolina Press

*To Pam*

Copyright © UNIVERSITY OF SOUTH CAROLINA 1987

Published in Columbia, South Carolina, by the
University of South Carolina Press

FIRST EDITION

Manufactured in the United States of America

Library of Congress Cataloging-in-Publication Data
Shortal, John F., 1951–
  Formed by fire.

  (American military history)
  Bibliography: p.
  Includes index.
  1. Eichelberger, Robert L.   2. Generals—United States
—Bibliography.   3. United States. Army—Biography.
4. World War, 1939–1945—Campaigns—Pacific Ocean.
I. Title.   II. Series: American military history
(Columbia, S.C.)
E745.E33S54   1987          87-19091
ISBN 0-87249-521-3

# Contents

Acknowledgments        vii

Introduction        ix

1.   The Seedbed of Command        1

2.   Buna: The Harsh Crucible of Combat        32

3.   Buna Avenged and Another Fire        62

4.   The Payoff in the Philippines        93

Epilogue: The Sunset Years        127

Abbreviations        131

Notes        133

Index        151

Illustrations

General Robert L. Eichelberger.        2

*Following page* 84
Demonstration at Fort Jackson for Winston Churchill.
Eichelberger at working lunch with staff.
General Douglas MacArthur.
Sir Thomas Blamey.
Brigadier General Cloval Byers.
General Walter Krueger.
Hollandia: Forty-first Division moves inland.
Eichelberger in front of world map.
General Swing briefs Eichelberger on road to Manila.

Eichelberger and Filipino guerrillas.
Tanks advance on Panay.
General Yamashita surrenders to Thirty-second Division.
MacArthur meets with press on 30 August 1945.
MacArthur, Halsey, and Eichelberger in prayer.


Maps

*Following page* 84
1.  Major Japanese War Objectives
2.  Papua, New Guinea
3.  Buna
4.  Hollandia
5.  Invasion of Luzon
6.  Final Allied Offensives, 28 February–1 July 1945

# Acknowledgments

IN THE COURSE OF PREPARING THIS BOOK, I HAVE INCURRED MANY DEBTS. I would like to thank Dr. Mattie Russell, Curator of Manuscripts, The Perkins Library, and her most able assistant Ellen Gartrell, for all their kindness and assistance. I would also like to thank Duke University for permission to quote from the Eichelberger Papers and to use the pictures contained in this volume. I am also indebted to Avery Press for allowing me to use the maps contained in this book. These maps are from the *Atlas for the Second World War: Asia and the Pacific*, General T. Griess, Series Editor, Avery Publishing Group, Inc., Garden City Park, New York. Reprinted by permission. I would also like to thank the United States Army Center of Military History for permission to use the United States Army photographs.

I am most grateful to Dr. Richard Sommers, Chief Archivist, United States Army Military History Institute, Carlisle Barracks, Pennsylvania, and Mrs. Marie Capps, Archivist, United States Military Academy Library, for their cheerful support and patience in assisting me with sources.

I am also indebted to Brigadier General Roy K. Flint, Dean of the Academic Board, United States Military Academy, who provided me with the opportunity to study in graduate school; to Colonels Robert Doughty, Paul Miles, and Kenneth Hamburger for their sage counsel and advice; to Colonel (Retired) Roger Nye for reading my manuscript and providing insightful suggestions; to Dr. Herb Bass and Waldo Heinrichs of Temple University for their assistance in improving my dissertation.

However, I could never have completed this work without the guidance and support of two men: Dr. Jay Luvaas of the Army War College, who introduced me to the subject of General Eichelberger and never grew impatient with my incessant questioning; and Dr.

Russell Weigley, of Temple University. If I attempted to elaborate on my debt to him, I would have to add another chapter to this book. Any errors contained in this work are mine alone.

# Introduction

*It is 1900 hours (7:00 P.M.) on 30 November 1942 at General Douglas Mac-*
*Arthur's forward headquarters, Port Moresby on the island of New Guinea.*

GENERAL DOUGLAS MACARTHUR AND THREE OF HIS STAFF OFFICERS STOOD
on the veranda of his headquarters building. The heat in Port
Moresby was oppressive and, despite a cool breeze blowing across
the bay, the shirts of all four men were drenched with perspiration.
The tension in the room was as heavy as the humidity and was
plainly evident on the face of each man.

These three were MacArthur's most trusted advisers. The first, his
air commander, General George Kenney, was short and feisty. He
was perhaps the most brilliant and innovative proponent of air
power in the United States Army in 1942. In the next three years his
creative imagination enabled him to write the book on the use of air
assets to support ground operations. But that was in the future; on
this day he had no answers for MacArthur's dilemma.

Major General Charles Willoughby, MacArthur's intelligence
officer, was also present. He was proud, aloof, and distant. His German background and his haughty attitude caused his contemporaries to compare him to a rigid, unfeeling Prussian officer. His
greatest attribute was his intense loyalty to MacArthur, which had
been cemented by service on Bataan. Willoughby could point out
problems to his boss, but he also had no solutions now.

The last officer present that evening was Lieutenant General
Richard K. Sutherland, MacArthur's chief of staff. He was intense,
efficient, and also a member of the so-called Bataan Gang. His primary value to MacArthur was his willingness to make the tough or
unpopular decisions MacArthur purposely avoided. He was ruthless
with those he considered weak or inefficient. That evening he had a

predictably ruthless recommendation for MacArthur—replace the leadership at the front.

The tension and fear that permeated that meeting resulted from the poor performance of the American soldiers fighting one-hundred miles away at Buna. MacArthur and his advisers had not yet become part of American military folklore. Their legendary strategic insight and island-hopping operations were in the future. That night MacArthur's reputation was based on the loss of the Philippines and the failure of his only offensive of the war—Buna. There he had sent in an untrained and ill-equipped division against Japanese regulars, and the offensive had been stymied.

MacArthur's options in solving this problem were severely limited. Logistically, New Guinea was far from the industrial might of the United States. There were no landing craft for an amphibious landing and the United States had no tanks in the region. MacArthur had only one other American division in Australia, but it was as untrained and ill-equipped as the division already at Buna. MacArthur was convinced, however, that the battle for Buna could still be won. Sutherland was correct; what was needed was a change of leadership. MacArthur believed that the right man could overcome all of these shortcomings and salvage a victory from the quagmire in New Guinea. Based upon Sutherland's recommendation, MacArthur sent to Australia for the only man in the theater he believed capable of obtaining that elusive victory—Lieutenant General Robert L. Eichelberger.

At 7:00 P.M. that evening General Eichelberger walked onto the veranda of MacArthur's headquarters. The conversation between MacArthur and his advisers ended abruptly and all eyes turned to Eichelberger. At first glance he certainly did not look like a savior. Six-foot-one-inch tall, he weighed 192 pounds, a good deal of which centered in his middle. His face was wrinkled and pleasant. He wore an awkward-looking saucer cap. He looked more like a school teacher than the dynamic commander needed to lead men in a desperate battle; but beneath the kindly exterior was a steel-like determination and the heart of a warrior.

MacArthur's greeting was terse and to the point. He briefly described the tactical situation at Buna and then, looking Eichelberger in the eye, gave the following order: "Take Buna or don't come back alive!" With that command Eichelberger was dismissed. The following morning Eichelberger departed for the front.

## Introduction

Who was he? What were his qualifications for command? What made him special? These were the questions asked not only by Mac-Arthur's staff, but also by the men on New Guinea whose lives would depend on his judgment.

Buna, a focal point in World War II for the United States Army, had a profound personal effect on Eichelberger. In the harsh crucible of combat, he developed his highly personalized leadership style. His creative intelligence enabled him to devise innovative tactics; and he became committed to a training philosophy that ensured that in future operations in the Pacific, American soldiers would be mentally and physically prepared for battle.

Eichelberger solved MacArthur's problem at Buna in just thirty-two days, but this was not the end of his heroics. Three more times MacArthur needed Eichelberger's services in order to save stalled operations. Building upon prior experiences, Eichelberger obtained victory for MacArthur in each instance. During these subsequent operations, Eichelberger developed a legendary reputation for success and earned a special role in MacArthur's operations as the Fireman of the Southwest Pacific.

# · 1 ·

# The Seedbed of Command

IN THE YEARS BEFORE WORLD WAR II, ROBERT LAWRENCE Eichelberger developed the leadership style that proved to be very effective in World War II. This style evolved through the myriad of assignments that an officer is given as his career takes him from second lieutenant to three-star general. In his formative years as an officer, Eichelberger developed a highly personalized method of command predicated on hard work, shared hardships with his officers and men, concern for those under his command, and a pervasive sense of humor.

Eichelberger was born on 9 March 1886 in Urbana, Ohio.[1] He was the youngest of the five surviving children of George Maley Eichelberger and Emma Ring Eichelberger. His father was a successful attorney-at-law. After graduating from Urbana High School in 1903, Robert Eichelberger entered Ohio State University with the intention of following in his father's footsteps and becoming a lawyer. His career plans changed, however, when Judge William R. Warnock, his father's law partner, was elected to Congress in November 1904. As a congressman, Judge Warnock was in a position to offer him an appointment to West Point, which Eichelberger quickly accepted.[2]

Eichelberger, as a sophomore in high school, had first seen the Corps of Cadets at the 1901 Pan-American Exposition in Buffalo,

General Robert L. Eichelberger (U.S. Army Photo).

and he had been profoundly impressed. Fifty years later he fondly recalled this first glimpse of the corps: "I watched them drill and parade and to this day my enthusiasm for the United States Military Academy is unabated."[3]

In June 1905 Eichelberger entered West Point as a member of the class of 1909. He found cadet life austere and markedly different from his experiences at Ohio State University.[4] Cadet Eichelberger encountered difficulties adjusting to cadet life. In his first year, his mathematics grades were so low that his father felt compelled to write to the superintendent of the Military Academy for assistance in obtaining tutoring for his son.[5] Cadet Eichelberger displayed the tenacity and drive that would be the hallmark of his career and he successfully overcame his academic problems. He graduated sixty-eighth in a class of 103. Although he was not a brilliant student, his outstanding leadership potential was evidenced by his selection as a cadet lieutenant—one of only twenty-six members of his class to be singled out for cadet command. The class of 1909 was one of the most distinguished in the history of West Point. Twenty-eight members of this class eventually became general officers, including General Jacob Devers, who stood thirty-ninth in his class and commanded the Sixth Army Group in World War II; General George Patton (46th), who commanded the Third Army, and General William Simpson (101st), who commanded the Ninth Army.[6]

Upon graduation from West Point, Eichelberger was commissioned a second lieutenant of infantry and assigned to I Company of the Tenth Infantry Regiment, which at that time was stationed at Fort Benjamin Harrison, Indiana. Eichelberger had selected the infantry because it possessed the greatest opportunity for promotion. He remained with this regiment for six years, in which time it moved first to Texas and then to Panama. During his formative years as an officer with the Tenth Infantry, Eichelberger learned a great deal about his profession and began to develop his own distinctive leadership style.

Shortly after arriving at Fort Benjamin Harrison, Second Lieutenant Eichelberger learned a seminal lesson of leadership that he never forgot and subsequently employed time and again in the Pacific in World War II: an officer must always lead by example if he is going to have the loyalty and support of his subordinates. Eichelberger described an incident that occurred on the regiment's annual 200-mile practice road march:

I had new shoes—the greatest mistake I made was not to
break in some uniform shoes on my summer's leave. As a
consequence, I limped in the last 100 miles and I had to fight
off suggestions that I ride in the ambulance. However, while
the soldiers were possibly a bit amused at my suffering, I felt
that I had their respect. Some officers rode in the ambulances
but in a long life time in the Army, that is one treatment to
which I never indulged myself.[7]

During these early years with the Tenth Infantry, Lieutenant Eichelberger observed the diverse leadership styles of his senior officers. From some officers he learned what not to do.

Some spent their off-duty hours, which were long, gambling
or in other forms of recreation. Some concentrated on the
post social life. Several thought it bright to lie in bed and
have the First Sergeant bring the morning report to their bed
to sign. I wonder what the First Sergeant thought of these
men. I never thought too highly of them then or into the
future.[8]

From other officers, especially his I Company commander—
Captain James B. Gowen—he observed those characteristics that
made an officer a successful leader. Captain Gowen was a handsome
officer who had graduated from West Point eleven years before Eichelberger. As a lieutenant, Gowen had been decorated with a Silver
Star for heroism in the Spanish-American War. His competence, professional attitude, and reputation for personal bravery made him
one of the most admired officers in the regiment. Gowen would go
on to a distinguished career in World War I and would retire as a
general officer.

Eichelberger believed that he learned much from Captain Gowen, because Gowen was a demanding officer who set high standards of performance and always led by personal example. Captain
Gowen did not play cards or drink away the evenings. He spent a
great deal of his time working with Eichelberger. Captain Gowen
was Eichelberger's first mentor. He taught Eichelberger the importance of paying attention to details and instilled in him a strong
sense of duty. Through his example, Eichelberger learned the importance of hard work and constant study in order to gain the knowledge and experience necessary to be a successful army officer.[9]
Eichelberger found that the company commanders who were suc-

cessful were those who possessed the characteristic of "looking after [their] men, the ones who were sick, the ones who had troubles at pay day . . . [and possessed an] intense interest in the men under their command from the first sergeants to the lowliest private."[10]

In addition to observing his superior officers, Eichelberger enhanced his tactical and technical proficiency by continued study at post schools. At that time junior officers received technical instruction from schools run by the regiment. He applied the majority of his off-duty time and energy to his studies rather than drinking, playing cards, and carousing. He did not do this because he was a prude but because he desired to be the best officer possible, and his study earned him certificates that could be used as exemptions from certain tests administered by the promotion boards.[11]

In March 1911, as tensions with Mexico increased, the Tenth Infantry Regiment was ordered to San Antonio, Texas, to become part of the "Maneuver Division" on the Mexican border. This tour of duty lasted from 11 March to 28 September 1911. During these six months the regiment lived in tents and conducted an intensive and difficult training program in order to prepare it for combat. During this period several of the less competent officers were relieved. As a result young Lieutenant Eichelberger received his first command, that of I Company, after Captain Gowen was moved to higher command. This was a notable accomplishment for a second lieutenant and spoke well for his reputation within the regiment.[12] His first command provided an excellent opportunity to test his early observations on leadership. Eichelberger also obtained a great deal of personal insight into the psyche of the American soldier. He later recalled:

> I found that enlisted men respond to the interests of officers. Naturally, a company of infantry will study its officers, their peculiarities and their weaknesses and probably they have had many a good laugh at an officer's expense. Pomposity, lack of interest, discipline by rank rather than personality—these qualities met quick response in lowered morale and often inefficiency.[13]

Lieutenant Eichelberger commanded I Company during its move from San Antonio, Texas, to Panama in late September 1911. The movement of a rifle company and all of its equipment was no mean task for a young officer, but he handled it well. While commanding this rifle company, through tactical exercises and mapping expeditions in Panama, he obtained valuable firsthand experience in the difficulties and peculiarities of jungle warfare and also gained new leadership insights—skills which would serve him well in the jungles of New Guinea in World War II.[14] During the course of one of these tactical drills in the Panamanian jungle, he learned a lesson on the importance of realistic and demanding training that had a profound effect on his future career. The incident occurred during a twenty-five-mile practice road march with full field equipment. Lieutenant Eichelberger was assigned to bring up the rear of the battalion to prevent straggling. Eichelberger related the incident as follows:

> In this work I was very much interested in Captain John B. Schoeffel, a big, husky, professional soldier. He had no sympathy for the soldier who quit. He wasn't bothered by the tears caused by fatigue. He told me that he felt that a man always had a lot left in him even when he felt he could go no further. The lessons I learned that day I never forgot. Captain Schoeffel was not my beau ideal of a fine officer but no men of his outfit fell by the wayside. I realized that the fact that we arrived with all our men in Las Cascadas in all that heat was due to the fact that these men were commanded by hard officers and noncommissioned officers of the Regular Army.[15]

In World War II as a division, corps, and army commander, Eichelberger many times had to push his men to go on when they felt they could not. He was drawing upon the lessons of the Panamanian jungles where he first learned the crucial balance between empathizing with the soldiers' problems and continuing to push them beyond their known limits. He also drew upon his experiences to ensure a challenging physical-fitness program and hard, tough, realistic training. He believed that the best way to ensure that a soldier would possess the courage and confidence necessary to accomplish the most difficult task in combat was to push him consistently to the limits of his capabilities. Physical fitness was also important for the soldiers in order to develop the right mental attitude to overcome fatigue and complete any assigned mission. From early on, in Panama, he had learned that "an untrained outfit would have disintegrated before that terrible hike was half over."[16]

The four years Eichelberger spent in Panama were not all hard work and strenuous training. At a party given in the home of Dr. William C. Gorgas, the man who eliminated yellow fever in the

Canal Zone, Eichelberger met his future wife. She was Emma Gudger, the daughter of Judge H. A. Gudger, the chief justice of the Canal Zone. After a brief courtship, they were married on 3 April 1913 at the Gudger home in Asheville, North Carolina. This marriage lasted for forty-eight years, until his death in 1961.[17] They had no children. Professor Jay Luvaas, who worked closely with both Robert and Emma Eichelberger while collecting the Eichelberger Papers for Duke University, wrote of the marriage:

> During their years together no couple could have been happier and more devoted. Eichelberger's admiration and affection are expressed in every letter and were evident in each gesture. Emma's staunch loyalty and agonizing concern for her husband's welfare were no less apparent, constituting throughout his career an unusual source of strength, and occasionally of worry.[18]

After their marriage, the young couple returned to Panama for two more years. However, because of the influence and position of Judge Gudger, they did not lead the life of the average second lieutenant and wife. Judge Gudger introduced them to many of the prominent social, political, and military personalities in the Canal Zone. Through these contacts both Judge Gudger and Eichelberger were able subtly to manipulate the latter's assignments over the next few years. Eichelberger learned from his father-in-law the importance of knowing socially men of influence and then how to use that influence to further his career.[19]

On 1 March 1915 the Eichelbergers departed Panama and were assigned to the Twenty-second Infantry Regiment at Fort Porter in Buffalo, New York. This assignment was an excellent example of Judge Gudger's ability to influence the lieutenant's career through his political contacts. The judge desired that the lieutenant and his wife be stationed on the East Coast and arranged the assignment through his long-time friend, Senator Lee S. Overman of North Carolina. Later the adjutant general of the army, who was surprised by the interest of a United States senator in the move of a lieutenant, questioned Eichelberger about the circumstances of that transfer. Eichelberger replied: "I had used no influence but I had a big suspicion that my father-in-law, Judge H. A. Gudger, of the Panama Canal Zone, had been active. While I did not know Senator Overman and had never seen him and was in entire ignorance of this change of station, I was happy indeed to know that I had a friend in Senator Overman."[20]

On 18 September 1915, after only six months at Fort Porter, Eichelberger was ordered to Fort Douglas, Arizona, to take the field with the Twenty-second Infantry Regiment. The Twenty-second was part of the Sixth Brigade—with the Eleventh, Fourteenth, and Eighteenth Infantry—of Brigadier General Thomas Davies's Third Provisional Division. Lieutenant Omar Bradley and Eichelberger's classmate, Edwin F. Harding, were also on the frontier with this brigade. Their mission was to patrol the Arizona-Mexico border and to protect the copper interests of the region from the raids of Francisco "Pancho" Villa. During the year in which he participated in this border duty, Eichelberger spent much of his time in the field, personally training his soldiers in the varied and almost limitless terrain of Arizona.[21]

The noteworthy occurrence during this tour of duty in Arizona was that Eichelberger had his first opportunity to observe a battle. This occurred in late October 1915, when Pancho Villa attacked the entrenchments of the American-backed Alvuro Obregon forces, loyal to President Venustiono Carranza, at Agua Priete, eighteen miles south of Douglas, Arizona. From an old slaughterhouse on the United States-Mexico border just 1,000 yards from Agua Priete, Eichelberger observed the bloody three-day battle. It was here that Eichelberger encountered a phenomenon that also influenced his leadership style. According to Eichelberger, "Officers were permitted and even encouraged to go to the international boundary and watch combat in progress."[22] However, many of the officers in the regiment remained at the Officers' Club playing cards and did not take advantage of this opportunity to observe the fighting firsthand. Eichelberger found this lack of interest on the part of his fellow officers reprehensible, because he believed that "an infantryman must prepare himself to lead troops in battle and where can one find out more than from actual conditions when bullets were flying?"[23]

Eichelberger encountered this attitude again and again throughout his career. He found that "many officers of varied ranks were willing to stay far from the whistle of a hostile bullet or bomb [and] fall back on the idea that an officer's life was too valuable to risk."[24] He contended with this attitude in Siberia and again in the Pacific in World War II. However, an essential characteristic of his leadership style continued to be the willingness to share the risks and discomforts of the soldiers in his command. He possessed what we would call today the "warrior spirit." He believed that personal courage was a prerequisite for command. In the Pacific in World War II, he would surround himself with officers who possessed the personal courage to lead by example and who consistently placed themselves in harm's way. Furthermore, he ruthlessly weeded out those officers who did not possess this attribute.

At the battle of Agua Priete, the Obregon forces with United States assistance were able to hold the entrenchments. The following March, Pancho Villa obtained revenge for this defeat by raiding the garrison at Columbus, New Mexico, which in turn led to the John J. Pershing Punitive Expedition. Eichelberger, however, did not get the opportunity to participate actively in the Pershing Expedition. In July 1916, after more than seven years of commissioned service, he was promoted to first lieutenant and transferred from the Mexican border to Kemper Military Academy in Boonesville, Missouri. At Kemper he was assigned the duties of professor of military science and tactics.[25]

This tour of duty was cut short by World War I. On 15 May 1917 Eichelberger was promoted to the rank of captain. He was then transferred to Fort Douglas, Utah, to command an infantry battalion in the Twentieth Infantry Regiment. After Eichelberger had been in command of this battalion for three months, the regiment was split because of the massive army expansion caused by the National Defense Act of 1916 and the war. This act doubled the strength of the army to 175,000 men and sixty-five infantry regiments. Captain Eichelberger was then transferred to Camp Pike, Arkansas, and again given command of a battalion; this time in the Forty-third Infantry Regiment. He commanded this battalion for five months before he was assigned to the General Staff in Washington.[26] It is highly probable that the influence of Judge Gudger succeeded in getting Eichelberger this choice assignment. He was thirty-one years old.

In the capital Captain Eichelberger was assigned to the staff of Brigadier General William S. Graves, the executive assistant to the chief of staff of the army. At fifty-three General Graves was a tall, heavyset soldier with piercing blue eyes. He had first established a reputation for efficiency and courage as an infantry officer in the Philippines during the Spanish-American War. In the decade before World War I, he had served in a variety of assignments on the General Staff in Washington, D.C. In this capacity he mastered the bureaucratic politics of the army and acquired the admiration and support of Secretary of War Newton Baker, and Army Chief of Staff Peyton C. March.

General Graves would be Eichelberger's mentor for twenty years and was very influential in molding Eichelberger's career. General Graves's staff consisted of only eight officers—one captain (Eichelberger), and seven colonels. This small group of officers fulfilled the role of what would today be called the G–1 or personnel section. Eichelberger was the assignments officer responsible for detailing all army officers above the rank of captain to overseas duty. This job provided Eichelberger with a unique opportunity. First, it allowed him to observe many of the senior officers in the army. He received a firsthand education on the best and the worst of the American officer corps. Eichelberger wrote: "Generals lined up in the hallway to see me and I remember feeling pride that most of them really wanted combat duty. Some asked to be relieved of overseas orders because of the nervousness of their wives. This I was glad to do because many were praying for the chance to fight."[27]

In addition to enhancing Eichelberger's study of the leadership traits of many senior officers, this assignment also afforded him the opportunity of gaining the attention of many influential officers in Washington through his dedication to duty and hard work. Eichelberger's desk was located directly outside General Graves's office and a short distance from the office of General Peyton C. March, the army chief of staff. Although Eichelberger was only a captain and was the most junior officer on General Graves's staff, he ended up handling responsibilities far in excess of his rank because "Some of the colonels felt it was not up to them to work too hard when they had a captain who seemed willing."[28]

This lack of professionalism by the senior members of General Graves's staff worked to Eichelberger's advantage. He executed all his assignments with the same relish and dedication he had displayed as a junior officer in the Tenth and Twenty-second Infantry. His professionalism in carrying out his duties and his willingness to take on more responsibility when others sought to avoid it greatly impressed both General Graves and General March. Thus, when the chief of staff gave Graves command of a division and overseas orders in July 1918, Captain Eichelberger was rewarded. General Graves directed Eichelberger to "cut orders assigning himself to Graves' staff." Furthermore, his confidence in Eichelberger was so great that the general permitted the young major to select the division he (Graves) would command. Eichelberger selected the Eighth Infantry Division, which was stationed in Palo Alto, California, and due to deploy to Europe in thirty days. Eichelberger selected this division because of its quick deployment date and his desire to get to France before the war ended.[29] Eichelberger did not realize it at the time, but his random selection of the Eighth Division was one of the most momentous decisions of his life.

Upon assuming command of the Eighth Infantry Division on 13 July 1918, General Graves assigned Major Eichelberger to the position of Division G–3 (operations officer). However, a month later, when the division's orders were changed from France to Siberia, Eichelberger was moved from the G–3 position to that of assistant chief of staff, G–2 (Intelligence). In this position, Eichelberger worked closely with General Graves and saw firsthand the problems his commander had in dealing with America's allies (France, Great Britain, and Japan) in Siberia.

Before examining Eichelberger's actions in Siberia and the impact of this mission on his personal leadership style and future career, some background on the purpose of this expedition is necessary. On 5 July 1918, when President Woodrow Wilson made the decision to intervene in Siberia, the Allied cause was in grave jeopardy. The German 1918 summer offensive had been dangerously successful. The Germans had smashed through the Allies' front lines, and the sound of artillery could be heard in Paris. As one noted historian has observed: "Wilson made the decision to intervene in Russia with American troops *before* the Germans were stopped in the Second Battle of the Marne (July 18 to August 6, 1918). It is also undeniable that the allies and the United States wanted to sustain military pressure on the Germans from the East."[30]

Marshal Ferdinand Foch, generalissimo of the Allied forces, desperately appealed to Wilson in July 1918 to send American troops to Siberia to bring about a restoration of the Eastern Front.[31] This second front would compel the Germans to transfer a sizable force from France to Russia. Foch hoped that this reassignment of troops would break the impetus of the German summer offensive. Thus Wilson's decision was made in light of severe military setbacks on the Western

Front, because he was convinced that the fate of democracy and civilization hung in the balance.

In addition to the poor military situation on the Western Front, Wilson was also influenced by the deteriorating relationship among the Allies. In the first five months of 1918, Wilson was obliged on six separate occasions to make formal replies rejecting Allied requests that he send an American expedition to Russia to create a diversion on the Eastern Front.[32] This friction, compounded by numerous prior incidents, created strained feelings between the United States and the Allies. Wilson had opposed Allied schemes and had

> insisted on being termed an associate rather than an ally. Wilson's insistence on the separateness of the armies of the United States at the front had been a serious point of friction with England and France. Furthermore, the United States had at first refused to send a military representative to participate in the activities of the Supreme War Council. In addition, there was disagreement over the terms of the peace settlement; Wilson was strongly opposed to the allies' eagerness for territory, and the secret treaties to acquire it were particularly difficult for him to accept.[33]

Thus, with the success of the German summer offensive of 1918, when the Allied Supreme War Council desperately urged an American intervention into Siberia as a diversion, Wilson felt compelled to act. He had turned down so many Allied requests that they were "beginning to feel that he was not a good associate, much less a good ally."[34] Therefore Wilson acquiesced to the Allies' wishes and agreed to send American troops to Siberia on 5 July 1918.

Another factor in this decision, although somewhat less important than the others, was Wilson's humanitarian feelings for the Czech Legion. The Czech Legion was "composed partly of men from Czech colonies in the former Russian Empire and partly of defectors from the Austro-Hungarian Army, this force consisting in all of some two divisions."[35] The only way this unit could get out of Russia while the war was still on was to move across Siberia and to be evacuated through Vladivostok. At the time that this Czech force commenced its trek across Siberia toward Vladivostok, a rumor reached the Allies that the new Soviet regime in Russia had released 600,000 German prisoners of war. These released prisoners were purportedly attempting to destroy the Czech Legion.

Woodrow Wilson's aide-memoire of 17 July 1918 clearly stated the objective of American intervention as "only to help the Czecho-Slovaks consolidate their forces and to get into successful cooperation with their Slavic kinsman."[36] American forces were not, however, to interfere with the political affairs of Siberia. Wilson, from the information he had received from the French and British, honestly believed that the American soldiers were assisting an "allied force, opposed by armed enemy nationals, to extract itself from a chaotic situation, in order to get to the Western Front."[37]

Eichelberger, from his vantage point as General Graves's Intelligence officer, found many of the French and British arguments used to induce Wilson to conduct the expedition to be false. First, he found that the Czech Legion en route to Vladivostok was in no danger. Rather, the Czech Legion, with French assistance, had seized the Trans-Siberian Railway and had attacked the Red forces at Irkutsk. Second, the "Austro-German Army Corps" composed of released prisoners of war was nonexistent. An unstated purpose of the expedition was Wilson's desire to curb Japanese militarism in the Far East. Eichelberger, however, was disenchanted with the British and French requests for American troops to keep an eye on the Japanese and protect the "Open Door," because in reality, he had found that they were the ones who were urging the Japanese into Siberia.[38]

Eichelberger was in Siberia from August 1918 to April 1920 as the assistant chief of staff (G–2), the military Intelligence officer for the expedition. For General Graves personally this was a very difficult and frustrating assignment. He was constantly berated by his French and British allies and the American State Department because he would not commit United States forces to the destruction of the Bolsheviks. When the State Department recognized Admiral Aleksandr Kolchak's White Russian government at Omsk, Graves refused to turn over weapons, clothing, and military equipment to them. He did this because "President Wilson's order to General Graves called upon him to bring economic relief to the Russian people and to maintain a position of neutrality between Russian factions—and Graves courageously and adamantly did so in the face of tremendous pressures." This led to the State Department's demand for Graves's relief. However, Wilson refused and was encomiastic in his support of Graves's performance.[39]

In this highly complex environment, fraught with hostility and intrigue among the Allies, Graves impressed Eichelberger with his integrity, courage, and honesty. During this period General Graves took daily walks with Eichelberger and, in frank discussions, used him as his sounding board. General Graves served as a father figure, teacher, and adviser to Eichelberger. On these long walks Graves and Eichelberger developed a close relationship. Eichelberger was the general's closest confidant, the one man whose discretion and loyalty he could always count on. In return for this service, General Graves provided Eichelberger a good deal of insight into the real machinations of the Army. He advised him on the unwritten rules of the army, who the most important people were, what cliques were rising in the army and why. In addition to teaching and guiding Eichelberger on how to succeed in the army, in the years after the war the general continued to advise Eichelberger and to use his influence to further his protégé's reputation and career. This experience was influential in molding Eichelberger's character and leadership style. He was still a young (aged thirty-three) infantry officer and was impressed by the moral example Graves set. Graves's professionalism was the model that Eichelberger sought to emulate throughout his career. The general's dedication to duty in attempting to execute his mission in a trying environment, while the Allies and the State Department undercut him, was admirable. General Graves set the moral tone for his command. His honesty and integrity in loyally obeying the spirit of President Wilson's instructions impressed the officers in his command. In the Pacific in World War II, Eichelberger drew on this experience in dealing with another highly complex situation, when his superiors in the rear envied him the publicity that resulted from success in battle.[40]

In addition to the educational benefit of his close association with General Graves, the Siberian Expedition had an important effect on Eichelberger's future career and character in other ways. First, it was his initial opportunity to test his philosophy of leadership, the product of ten years of observation, in the harsh crucible of combat. As Intelligence chief, Lieutenant Colonel Eichelberger could easily have remained at division headquarters, but he was convinced that it was his responsibility to go forward with the soldiers to see the terrain as it actually existed and not simply to stick pins in a map at division headquarters.[41] He consistently sought to gain combat experience in order to improve himself professionally, to share in the hardships and dangers of the enlisted men, and to know by personal observation what was going on at the front.

Eichelberger's personal courage and aggressive leadership were so extraordinary on three separate occasions that he was eventually awarded a Distinguished Service Cross (the nation's second highest award for gallantry in action). Excerpts from his Distinguished Service Cross citation give ample evidence of the determination and will to win on the battlefield of this young officer. On 28 June 1919, "at the imminent danger of his own life, he entered the partisan lines and effected the release of one American officer and three enlisted men in exchange for a Russian prisoner." On 2 July 1919 at the village of Novitskaya, "an American platoon detailed to clear hostile patrols from a commanding ridge was halted by enemy enfilading fire, seriously wounding the members of the patrol. He, without regard to his own safety and armed with a rifle, voluntarily covered the withdrawal of the platoon." Then on 3 July 1919 he again displayed great coolness under fire and dynamic personal leadership when "an American column being fired upon when debouching from a mountain pass he voluntarily assisted in establishing the firing line, preventing confusion, and, by his total disregard for his own safety, raised the morale of the American forces to a high pitch."[42]

Equally important as the honing of Eichelberger's leadership skills, the Siberian Expedition affected his career in another way. Instead of experiencing the rigors of trench warfare on the Western Front, as did most of his contemporaries, he gained valuable first-hand experience with Japanese militarism. In his twenty months in Siberia Eichelberger participated in numerous operations with the Japanese. He was particularly impressed by the discipline and training of the individual Japanese soldier.

"I had marched with the Japanese a number of times and their patrolling was meticulous." When the Japanese were fired upon, "all points within rifle fire of the main body were carefully covered." Eichelberger also observed that compared to American soldiers, the Japanese were "decidedly better trained and disciplined." Furthermore, if given "equally good leadership . . . the Japanese would defeat us in battle."[43] Eichelberger's observations of the Japanese had convinced him that "Japanese militarism had as its firm purpose the conquest of all Asia."[44]

After Eichelberger departed Siberia on 1 April 1920, his knowledge of the Japanese continued to have an effect on his career. His reputation as an expert on the Japanese military machine dictated his assignments for the next four years. Later, his intimate knowledge of the Japanese army was of invaluable importance to him in the Pacific in World War II. To utilize his acute appreciation for the capabilities of the Japanese army, he was assigned to the Philippine Department as the G–2 (Intelligence officer). He served in this capacity from May to October 1920, and greatly impressed General Francis J. Kernan, the commanding general of the Philippine Department, with his dedication to duty and attention to detail. At age sixty-two, General Kernan was at the end of a long and distinguished career in the United States Army. Despite thinning white hair and a salt-and-pepper mustache, his powerful physique and handsome face gave him the aura of a much younger man. In the Spanish-American War he had been decorated for gallantry in action at Manila. During World War I General John J. Pershing had selected him to set up the logistical support for the entire American Expeditionary Force. General Kernan wanted to help Eichelberger because he saw in the young officer many of the characteristics that had made him successful in combat. General Kernan wrote the War Department that Eichelberger's "duties were performed in a thorough and conscientious manner and indicated marked intelligence, efficiency and hard work."[45]

However, on 11 October 1920 Eichelberger was relieved as G–2 because he had not appeared on the list of General Staff Eligible Officers. General Graves and General Kernan, who both considered Eichelberger a protégé, were upset by this omission and protested to Washington. General Graves wrote Eichelberger to advise him that "the eligible list was prepared by officers whose services were in France . . . No officer on this board had knowledge of your exceptionally valuable services during the World War . . . and that is why you were relieved."[46] Nevertheless, General Kernan so valued Eichelberger's knowledge and experience with the Japanese that he then sent him to Tientsin, China, to establish a G–2 (Intelligence) section there.

After ten months in Tientsin, in August 1921 Eichelberger returned to the United States. He was assigned to the Far Eastern Section of the General Staff's Military Intelligence Division, where he was responsible for China, the Philippines, and Siberia. He remained in this position for three years, and through continuous study of the region during this time he bolstered his reputation in

Washington and throughout the army as an expert on the Japanese.[47]

In his three-year tour with the Military Intelligence Division, Eichelberger's efficiency, attention to detail, and capacity for hard work continued to bring him the notice and respect of his superiors. Every assignment he was given, he executed to the best of his ability. In 1922 the G–2 of the army complimented Eichelberger "on the efficient way in which he performed [his] duty" during the course of the Limitation of Armaments Conference in Washington.[48] His reputation as an expert on the Japanese expansion in the Far East earned him an assignment as liaison officer with the Chinese delegation to the arms-reduction talks in the post-World War I years. In 1923 his performance in handling matters relating to the funeral of President Warren G. Harding brought him commendations from President Calvin Coolidge, Secretary of War John W. Weeks, and Deputy Chief of Staff of the Army Major General John Hines. General Hines wrote: "Your executive ability, tact and painstaking follow-up undoubtedly relieved the War Department from embarrassing complaints and materially assisted in coordination between the War and Navy Departments."[49]

The army was a very trying profession in the post-World War I era. Russell Weigley, the noted military historian, has written that "America in the 1920's was dedicated not only to the dream that wars had ended forever, but even more strongly to the more prosaic fetish of economy in government."[50] A penurious government had by 1922 reduced the regular army from 280,000 to 125,000 men.[51] War seemed far away, and infantry battalions became so depleted that they turned out for drill with fewer than forty men.

This reduction also affected Eichelberger, who in July 1920 was reduced in rank to major, a career disappointment for an ambitious, hard-working officer. It seemed entirely possible that he would retire a lieutenant colonel. The army of this era had only twenty brigadier generals, and most did not achieve this rank until the age of fifty-nine or sixty. Furthermore, the rank of major general was usually given as a reward for good service shortly before retirement.[52]

In 1924 Eichelberger carefully evaluated his career opportunities and decided to transfer from the infantry to the Adjutant General's Corps. This turned out to be a wise move. As an infantry officer he had successfully commanded at the company and battalion levels. As a staff officer he had been the G–3 (operations officer), G–2 (Intelligence officer), and the assistant chief of staff of an infantry division. He had conducted operations in the jungles of Panama, the deserts of Arizona, and the wastelands of Siberia.

Additionally, Eichelberger had a distinguished war record; he was one of nine officers in the United States Army who had been awarded both the Distinguished Service Cross and the Distinguished Service Medal. Yet the chances of his reaching the rank of general as an infantry officer seemed remote. He believed the opportunity to become a general appeared better in the Adjutant General's Corps. In the army of that era, the adjutant general (AG) was second to the chief of staff in importance, and the AG of the army, General Robert C. Davis, had been greatly impressed by the efficiency and quality of Eichelberger's work since he had returned to Washington. General Davis, a classmate of Eichelberger's First Company commander, James B. Gowen, had also had a distinguished career in the infantry before transferring to the Adjutant General's Corps. He had twice been awarded the Silver Star for gallantry in action during the Spanish-American War. In World War I he had served as the adjutant general of the American Expeditionary Force in France. General Davis promised Eichelberger that if he made this transfer, he would send Eichelberger immediately to the Command and General Staff School (as it then was called); and if he stood high enough in the class, to the Army War College.[53]

In July 1924 Eichelberger transferred to the Adjutant General's Corps. General Davis kept his word, and on 7 September 1925 Eichelberger entered the Command and General Staff School at Fort Leavenworth, Kansas. As General Omar Bradley stated in his autobiography, selection for this school was a great honor. Furthermore, those officers who graduated and subsequently discharged their duties satisfactorily were virtually assured promotion to colonel before retirement. There were 248 officers in the class of 1926, many of whom went on to fame in World War II: Dwight D. Eisenhower, Joseph W. Stilwell, Leonard Gerow, Joseph T. McNarney, and William Rupertus, to name a few.[54] As this list might indicate, the competition to finish high academically was fierce. Omar Bradley believed that "since the assumption had taken root that a high grade at the Command and General Staff School would almost insure promotion to colonel or general, for too long the competition at the School had been literally killing. Some students who failed to score high had nervous breakdowns or committed suicide." Prior to the Command and General Staff School, most of the officers had attended service schools that provided a year's preparation for the rigors of the Command and General Staff School by using "old C&GS School problems to instruct the students."[55] This was an accepted practice, and the faculty of the Command and General Staff School believed themselves "held back by the fact that too many students coming here have not had the advantage of the special Service Schools' training."[56] Because of his branch transfer to the AG, Eichelberger was not afforded the opportunity of attending a service school prior to Leavenworth. Yet he overcame this handicap through his usual quest for knowledge and dedication to duty.

"The class at Leavenworth was divided into committees of about 20, and each committee was assigned two instructors whose duty it was to assist in every way possible the members of the committee to which assigned."[57] These committees were arranged alphabetically, and Eichelberger spent the year sitting next to Major Dwight D. Eisenhower, who was the Number One graduate in the class. Eichelberger graduated on the Distinguished Graduates List (top 25 percent), which was a considerable accomplishment for an AG officer who did not have the benefit of a service school preparation.[58]

General Davis was so pleased with Eichelberger's performance that he appointed him to be the adjutant general of the Command and General Staff School at Fort Leavenworth. Eichelberger served in this assignment until 8 July 1929, when he was selected to attend the Army War College. Eichelberger's selection for attendance at the War College marked him as the rising star in the Adjutant General's Corps. In fact, 52 percent of all War College graduates in the classes from 1920 to 1940 became general officers.[59] In the Army War College class of 1930, forty out of eighty-four officers became general officers in World War II.[60] Eichelberger described the selection process as follows:

> One out five went to Leavenworth and of those, about half were selected to be on the General Staff Eligible List and a few were selected to go to the Army War College. A comparatively small number of officers were selected to go to the Army War College, maybe one-fifth as many as went to Leavenworth so it is apparent there was a lot of selection before one ended up at the War College.[61]

The year Eichelberger spent at the War College was beneficial for two reasons. First, his hard work brought him to the attention of Major General William D. Connor, the commandant of the Army War College. At fifty-six General Connor was one of the most brilliant officers in the American army. He was six feet tall and did not possess an ounce of fat on his body. Although he was completely bald, his face was as taut and unwrinkled as that of a thirty-year-old. He had been in combat in Spain, the Philippine Insurrection, and World War I. He had displayed great personal courage on numerous battlefields and had twice been decorated with the Silver Star. General Connor was a dedicated professional whose sponsorship had a profound influence on Eichelberger's career. Second, the War College provided Eichelberger an excellent opportunity to study and reflect on his profession.

Eichelberger had been away from the infantry for five years, and this school enabled him to gain valuable experience in handling large units. The War College emphasized command throughout its course by using war games and map exercises that challenged the tactical decision-making process of its students.[62] These games provided good preparation for World War II in view of the fact that the active army was practically nonexistent in the 1930s. Furthermore, army officers had little opportunity to gain experience and skill in commanding large forces, and the War College provided the only substitute.[63] The flexibility and tactical innovativeness that were the hallmark of Eichelberger's World War II operations were developed during these exercises and his constant study of military history at the War College.

A brief tour at the War Department in Washington followed his graduation from the Army War College in June 1930. Eichelberger was then selected as adjutant general and secretary of the Academic Board at the United States Military Academy at West Point. In this position Eichelberger worked closely with General William Connor, who was now the academy's superintendent.

The AG position at West Point was considered an important one in the Adjutant General's Corps, and Eichelberger's assignment signified that his career was being closely monitored. In 1933 Brigadier General James F. McKinley, the adjutant general of the United States Army, requested Eichelberger as his executive officer. General William Connor was reluctant to release him, and he wrote of Eichelberger: "I have a very high regard for him personally and for his ability, which feelings I gathered from your statement you share with me. These are not times in which one should hold back in the harness and I feel that we ought to have the best man in Washington to deal with the situations that are available in the Army."[64]

Although this transfer did not take place, the following year General McKinley, with General Connor's support, sponsored Eichelberger for an even better job—secretary to the General Staff. Both these officers considered Eichelberger a protégé and sought to further his career. General McKinley's opinion of Eichelberger was reflected in the following words: "I think [it] the best job there is for a Lieutenant Colonel or Colonel on the War Department General Staff . . . I am very happy about it because it will bring you in very close contact with all the higher-ups, which will mean a lot to you in the future."[65]

On 1 July 1935 Eichelberger was assigned to duty as the secretary to the General Staff in the War Department. At that time General Douglas MacArthur was the chief of staff of the army and Major General George S. Simonds was the deputy chief of staff. Although Eichelberger had never met General MacArthur, his record at the Command and General Staff School, as adjutant general at Fort Leavenworth, and as adjutant general at West Point had impressed many senior officers in the army. General MacArthur's aide, Major Eisenhower, who had known Eichelberger well at Leavenworth, strongly recommended him. Furthermore, General McKinley wanted an AG officer to have this position, and with General Connor's assistance he was successful in obtaining it for Eichelberger.[66]

Eichelberger worked closely with MacArthur during the last three months of MacArthur's term as chief of staff. It was Eichelberger's duty as secretary to the General Staff to gather up daily all the staff studies of the General Staff and to brief MacArthur. Thus the very nature of his job brought him into close contact with MacArthur, who confided a great deal of information to him to ensure continuity in the office of the chief of staff when he departed. This experience gave Eichelberger the opportunity to observe the thought process and personality of General MacArthur, which proved to be an invaluable asset in the Pacific in World War II.[67]

On 2 October 1935 General Malin Craig became the new chief of staff of the army. General Craig was sixty years old in 1935. Tall and razor-thin, with gray hair and thick wire-rimmed eyeglasses, he looked more like a college professor than a professional soldier. However, he was a man of action who had participated in bloody fighting in Cuba, China, and France. Craig has been described as "a Pershing protégé, with qualities of hardheaded realism and determination reminiscent of Pershing himself . . . But he accomplished much at a time when he still had little support, and mainly he was a success because he was uncommonly foresighted and capable."[68] He was a skillful politician who knew his way around the bureaucratic labyrinth of the nation's capital. General Craig had the difficult mission of expanding the United States Army during the last years of the depression.

Eichelberger soon developed a close relationship with General Craig. They ate lunch daily in the chief's office, during which the general confided in Eichelberger many of the frustrations he encountered while trying to improve the army's military readiness. In addition, at these meetings General Craig sought to advise and counsel Eichelberger on his future career. He instructed Eichelberger on the bureaucratic politics within the army. He identified those officers within the army who were on the rise and who could benefit his career later on. The general, in the twilight of his career, tried to pass his knowledge about the army on to Eichelberger. Until his death in 1945 General Craig was Eichelberger's greatest mentor and supporter. He used all of his influence to sponsor Eichelberger for positions of increasing responsibility. Even when Eichelberger was in MacArthur's shadow in the Pacific, Craig ensured his protégé was not forgotten in Washington.[69]

Eichelberger's reputation for efficiency resulted in several senior officers requesting his services. General William D. Connor requested his appointment as commandant of cadets at West Point in 1936. Connor stated that "In my opinion, the characteristics which are essential are youth, energy, intelligence, balanced judgement and a sympathetic understanding of young men."[70] Connor also believed that mature judgment, which resulted from experience in command of troops, and skillful administrative ability were important qualifications and he recommended six officers in order of preference:

1. Lt. Col. R. L. Eichelberger
2. Captain Frederick B. Butler, CE
3. Lt. Col. J. L. Devers, FA

4. Lt. Col. D. D. Eisenhower, Infantry
5. Lt. Col. G. S. Patton, Cavalry
6. Lt. Col. C. P. Stearns, Cavalry[71]

General Craig, after several discussions with Eichelberger, allowed him to make the final decision in this matter. Eichelberger chose to remain in the key position as secretary to the General Staff.

In the late 1930s developments in Germany convinced Eichelberger that war was approaching. Three important general officers, recognizing Eichelberger's talent for command, advised him to transfer back to the infantry. General Connor had written in Eichelberger's West Point Efficiency Report that in time of war he should "command an Infantry Division."[72] In 1936 Connor urged: "I would make the move if I were you at the earliest moment that I could and, as you intimate, use the next two years to let the few who would notice it (his transfer from the AG Corps) have time to forget it."[73] Brigadier General George S. Simonds agreed: ". . . with your Infantry background, your war service, and the schools, there is no doubt as to your qualifications to be a combat commander. A refresher course at Benning and a tour of duty with troops as soon as possible after expiration of your present detail should put you in the running with other Infantry Colonels."[74] General Craig also advised him that "You ought to be with troops in case of a war."[75]

Weighing against this decision was Eichelberger's fear of offending General McKinley, the AG of the army. The general felt a distinct pride in Eichelberger's accomplishments and did not want him to transfer to the infantry. Eichelberger believed that he owed a great deal to the AG Corps, since it had sent him to Command and General Staff School and the War College. General Davis and General McKinley had also selected him for key jobs and used their influence to enhance Eichelberger's reputation. They had been his mentors and had advised, guided, protected, and sponsored him for fourteen years. Nevertheless, in the summer of 1937 he decided to transfer back to the infantry.[76] However, General Craig felt that he was so essential that he kept Eichelberger in the position of secretary to the General Staff for fifteen months after the branch transfer.

In August 1938 Eichelberger was promoted to full colonel. Two months later he left Washington to attend a short course at the Infantry School before assuming command of a regiment. Brigadier

General George C. Marshall, now the deputy chief of staff, had selected him to straighten out a problem regiment—the Thirtieth Infantry stationed in San Francisco. This assignment reflects the confidence that General Craig and General Marshall had in his abilities. Although he had been out of the infantry for more than fourteen years, they were entrusting him with one of the few peacetime regiments and, at that, with one suffering from severe problems.[77]

The problem in the Thirtieth Infantry resulted mainly from the callous attitude of Colonel Irving J. Phillipson, the regimental commander, in dealing with his subordinates. Eichelberger found the morale in the regiment poor. One manifestation of low morale was that the officers of the regiment were boycotting the Officers' Club. Eichelberger found General Marshall's assessment of the situation to be correct: "The officers hate him [Phillipson] and his wife assists him in raising hell with the Regiment."[78]

Colonel Eichelberger met with success in straightening out the Thirtieth Infantry Regiment through his commonsense approach to leadership. Realizing that San Francisco offered a great deal of social opportunities for his officers and men, he allowed his subordinates to spend their off-duty time in that city, adamantly refusing to make the regimental Officers' Club the center of social life. This realistic attitude dramatically improved the camaraderie and morale of the officers. To improve the morale of the junior officers and enlisted men, Eichelberger made the Thirtieth Infantry a regiment to be proud of. He established clear goals and enforced high standards. With Eichelberger's support, the regimental boxing, pistol, and rifle teams won army-wide championships. In addition Eichelberger developed his subordinates. He gave his junior officers and noncommissioned officers (NCOs) responsibility and created an environment where they could be creative but still have the freedom to fail. Several of these officers and NCOs from the Thirtieth Regiment would be called on in the Pacific, by Eichelberger, to accomplish difficult missions in combat.[79]

However, it was Eichelberger's tough, demanding training program that was most successful in improving the regiment's morale as well as increasing its combat efficiency. As the danger of war heightened, there were more and more maneuvers that kept the Thirtieth Infantry constantly on the move between San Francisco, Fort Lewis, Washington, and Fort Ord near Monterey, California.[80] During the course of these maneuvers, Eichelberger displayed great concern for the welfare of his enlisted men, a concern that paid handsome dividends in morale and efficiency. Eichelberger's understanding of human nature and concern for his troops led him to start every day in which they were in the field by being out with his soldiers at breakfast. He summed up his philosophy as follows:

> I found that my constant interest in the comfort of my men paid off in a large measure of devotion and loyalty from the enlisted men and added interest on the part of the officers. No junior officers are going to realize that the Colonel of the Regiment is out in the rain or sleet watching the service of meals to troops down the line in the winter without getting out themselves. Under those conditions with everybody putting their shoulders to the wheel, there is little or no grumbling from the soldier. This is a far cry from the old time officers who used to let the old First Sergeant bring the morning report to them in their bunks or beds.[81]

In January 1940 Eichelberger and the Thirtieth Infantry participated in maneuvers at Fort Ord. Eichelberger was given command of several National Guard units as well as the Thirtieth Infantry. His mission was to defend Monterey Bay from an amphibious assault. The Third Infantry Division (minus the Thirtieth Infantry Regiment) was the invading force. General Marshall, now army chief of staff, personally observed the operation. The conduct of the Thirtieth Infantry as a result of Eichelberger's demanding training program was exemplary. In maneuvers later that spring, Eichelberger was selected as the acting division commander of the Third Infantry Division. He wrote of this period: "I consider the years 1939–1940 with all the attendant maneuvers extending from Paso Robles to Fort Lewis, Washington as the most valuable preparatory years of my life. I was under constant observation and no officer ever reported on me who did not recommend me to become a General Officer."[82]

In October 1940 Eichelberger was promoted to brigadier general. This advancement was in part attributable to his success in turning around the troubled Thirtieth Infantry to General Marshall's satisfaction, coupled with the regiment's outstanding performance in the 1940 maneuvers. Although General Craig had favorably sponsored Eichelberger to Marshall, it was Eichelberger's leadership and excellent results with the Thirtieth Regiment that finally earned him General Marshall's esteem and respect. In the future General Marshall was to be influential in the selection of Eichelberger for division, corps, and army command.[83]

In October 1940, after his promotion to brigadier general, Eichelberger was ordered to West Point as superintendent. En route there from San Francisco, he stopped in Washington to receive a briefing from General Marshall, who had just closed the Army War College and had reduced the Command and General Staff School to a short course of several months. There were serious discussions in Washington of reducing West Point to a one-year course as had been done during World War I. For the next fifteen months, Eichelberger's major mission from Marshall was to prevent this reduction in the course of instruction at West Point.[84] Eichelberger's attitude was summed up in this letter to Major General Francis H. Wilby:

> The action of Annapolis, in reducing its course, is
> understandable in view of the well-known desire of the Navy
> to have Annapolis graduates dominate that service. This latter
> we cannot imitate. We can only furnish a small leaven to a
> very large Army but that leaven should be one so fine that its
> value will be self-evident to everyone. During World War I,
> West Point was thoroughly ruined and the evidences of that
> catastrophe were still most evident when I returned in 1931.[85]

To prevent such a reduction, Eichelberger sought to change West Point's public image and modernize its training. To change the public image, he eliminated all photographs of cadets riding horses and picnicking with their girlfriends. Instead, he attempted to stress the role of West Point in preparing young officers to lead men in combat, by distributing photographs of cadets conducting field maneuvers. He constantly emphasized to the press that West Point's mission was to provide future combat leaders.[86]

General Eichelberger also modernized the training at West Point better to prepare the cadets for modern mechanized warfare. He decreased the hours of instruction devoted to equitation, close-order drill, and ceremonies, and concomitantly introduced the study of German and insisted that the cadets receive instruction in the German campaigns of 1939–40. He increased the amount of military instruction on air forces, armored forces, anti-aircraft defense, anti-tank defense, infantry heavy weapons, and motor transport operations. In an attempt to provide the most practical and realistic training for the cadets, he sent the entire first class to Fort Dix, New Jersey, to participate in a field training exercise with the Forty-fourth Infantry Division and then to Fort Benning, Georgia, and Langley Field, Virginia, for instruction on the most modern equipment.

Recognizing the importance of the United States Army Air Corps in future military operations, Eichelberger introduced an air program at West Point by purchasing Stewart Field, in nearby Newburgh, New York, for that instruction.[87] All of these changes were made with one goal in mind: "All our publicity, the changes in the curriculum, the increase of hours for military training, the refresher course, etc., and particularly the new air program, were based in no small part on my desire for the preservation of West Point."[88] Through his efforts General Eichelberger successfully ensured that West Point was not reduced again to a one-year course, and he postponed its reduction to a three-year course for some time.[89]

General Eichelberger also attempted to instill within the cadets his intense interest in his profession and his equally competitive desire to be the very best at everything he undertook. He believed that the football team was an important instrument in teaching the cadets about life and competition. On his first day as superintendent at West Point, he saw the University of Pennsylvania football team crush army by a score of 48 to 0. He wrote of the experience:

> The cadets were wonderful losers; they continued to cheer
> their team to the opponent's last touchdown. But I felt they
> deserved a team which would teach them to be good winners.
> I still think, insofar as Army officers are concerned, that the
> concept of graceful losing can be overdone; in combat
> warfare there may be no game next week.[90]

Eichelberger set out to rectify this situation and produce a winning team at West Point with his usual enthusiasm. He found that the army weight standards, as set by the surgeon general, and poor coaching were at fault. For example, the official army weight standard dictated that a cadet of six feet could weigh only 160 pounds plus or minus ten percent. All requests for waivers were adamantly refused by the surgeon general. Eichelberger, who had learned the ropes of army politics from General Craig, enlisted the cooperation of Major General Edwin "Pa" Watson, President Roosevelt's aide and secretary, in revising the weight regulations. He also hired Earl

Blaik, the successful Dartmouth coach, as West Point's new head coach. With these actions, "the long victory drought on the highlands above the Hudson came to an end."[91]

In July 1941 Eichelberger was promoted to major general. Although Marshall wanted him to leave West Point and take a division immediately, General Watson blocked this transfer for six months. This was a difficult period for Eichelberger, since both men were very influential and he could not afford to offend either one. The Japanese attack on Pearl Harbor, however, ended this dilemma. Immediately after the attack, Eichelberger requested a transfer from West Point, which was granted on 5 January 1942.[92]

Eichelberger's next assignment required him to organize and train for combat the Seventy-seventh Infantry Division at Fort Jackson, South Carolina. This division was composed mainly of recruits from New York, New Jersey, and New England. To create an entire division from scratch was an enormous task, which tested Eichelberger's leadership and management skills to their limit, but he attacked this mission with his usual enthusiasm. He set high standards and demanded total commitment from his officers. He

> directed that officers sleep in camp three nights a week and
> that did not mean they could go on to their families in early
> evening and then back to sleep in camp. It means a period of
> 36 continuous hours 3 times a week. This gave us a chance to
> have schools at night under the direct supervision of officers.
> It enabled me, sleeping in camp, to be out before reveille,
> with what the soldiers dubbed the "Dawn Patrol."[93]

As was the case in the Thirtieth Infantry, this system brought all officers in the division into the "Dawn Patrol." With Eichelberger setting a personal example of a fifteen-hour work day, the training and discipline of the division progressed rapidly. He personally spent every night in camp and inspected all training from sunup to sunset and then attended the night classes given to the soldiers.[94]

This was evidenced by the official Seventy-seventh Division history, which stated:

> The men could not help seeing that the officers were working
> on a longer, tougher schedule than the one they were
> following. This was particularly true in the companies and
> batteries. Most of the platoon leaders, at the start, knew very
> little more than the men, and less than some of the cadre

sergeants; but the officers had responsibilities. By Division order, every company officer was required to spend eight to ten hours with his unit on the training field. Most of that time he was teaching what he had probably learned only the night before. Also by Division order, each officer attended a two-hour school three or four nights a week . . . It is understandable that at least one capable sergeant refused to go to Officer Candidate School because he "would not put up with the hell my lieutenants are getting here."

Eichelberger told his troops "we shall have thorough training and hard work, the methods used by all successful armies." He reminded them that "this will be no joy ride or picnic."[95]

Eichelberger's reputation for efficiency and hard work was enhanced by the reports prepared by distinguished visitors. In early June Vice Admiral Lord Louis Mountbatten inspected the Seventy-seventh Division and wrote:

> Of the many remarkable and inspiring sights I saw on the tour the one that made the greatest impression was the sight of the 77th Division marching by in review order like veterans. The fact that this state of efficiency can be reached in eight weeks has completely revolutionized my ideas of the future.[96]

Lord Mountbatten informed Winston Churchill of the division's efficiency, achieved after only eight weeks of training, and the prime minister then requested the opportunity to inspect this division personally. Churchill was skeptical of the United States' ability to raise an army of sufficient size and quality to conduct a cross-Channel invasion in the foreseeable future. General Marshall assigned Eichelberger the task of putting on a corps demonstration (there were three divisions at Fort Jackson) to convince Churchill of the American army's capabilities.[97]

On 18 June 1942 Eichelberger was made the I Corps commander; comprising the Seventy-seventh, Thirtieth, and Eighth divisions. The following day General Marshall gave him the mission of conducting a demonstration for Winston Churchill. He had only seventy-two hours to prepare this demonstration. In addition to Winston Churchill, Secretary of War Henry L. Stimson, General Marshall, Field Marshal Sir John Dill, and Field Marshal Sir Alan Brooke attended. Despite the short notice, the demonstration was a complete success. It reconfirmed Marshall's confidence in Eichelberger and impressed Churchill with America's ability to mass-produce quality divisions. General Marshall commented that he was confident of America's ability to train a citizen army for modern warfare. "The training shown by these new soldiers has lifted a weight off my shoulders equalled only by the winning of the recent battle in the Pacific [Coral Sea]."[98]

In early August 1942, while observing the amphibious training of the Ninth Division in Chesapeake Bay, Eichelberger received an abrupt call to return to Washington. When he arrived, General Marshall informed him that I Corps was to proceed to Australia. On 20 August 1942, after ten days of briefing and preparation, Eichelberger and his staff departed for Australia.[99] Eichelberger did not realize it at the time, but he had a "rendezvous with destiny."

Eichelberger was fifty-six years old, and in thirty-three years of commissioned service he had progressed from a novice to a major general. During these years he had developed into the consummate professional soldier. He was an excellent leader, manager, trainer, tactician, and warrior. He was physically fit and possessed the stamina to lead men in combat. His most outstanding characteristics were his tenacity, capacity for hard work, and desire to be the best at any assigned mission.

Eichelberger had been very fortunate in his early years in attracting some brilliant officers as mentors. Captain Gowen, his initial Company commander, had taught him to establish goals and set high standards and then to work hard to achieve them throughout his career. This fundamental lesson enabled him to impress General Graves in Washington and Siberia. General Graves was an important role model to Eichelberger. He taught Eichelberger about the bureaucratic politics of the army and how to succeed within the organization. Furthermore, Graves guided, advised, sponsored, and protected Eichelberger for the rest of his career. Through Graves's tutelage and his own efficiency, Eichelberger impressed General Kernan and General Davis. Both these officers guided and advised Eichelberger and helped his career. General Davis and General McKinley sponsored Eichelberger to important schools and prestige jobs culminating in that of secretary to the General Staff. Finally, General Craig taught Eichelberger much about the army. He also helped get Eichelberger back into the infantry and then sponsored him in commands of increasing responsibility.

Eichelberger's ability to impress his superiors was due to his own talent and hard work. He constantly studied his profession and was an excellent leader and manager. He knew how to establish goals, enforce high standards, and develop subordinates. In Panama, Mexico, Siberia, San Francisco, and Fort Jackson, experience had taught him that soldiers respected hardworking officers who were willing to share their dangers and discomforts. His forte was that he truly cared about people. He had a sincere concern for the comforts and well-being of his men. In the Tenth, Twenty-second, Twentieth, Forty-third, and Thirtieth regiments he always looked out for the welfare of his men. Yet at the same time he was a demanding troop trainer who believed in difficult and realistic training. He sought to give his troops the best possible chance to survive in combat, and he did this by pushing his soldiers to accomplish results that they believed beyond their limit. His success could be measured by the outstanding progress in the Thirtieth Regiment and in the Seventy-seventh Division.

Eichelberger, by constantly studying his profession and seeking to experience new phenomena, had developed a flexible and innovative mind. He had learned a great deal about tactics at the War College and in command of a regiment and a division. Most important, the enemy he knew best and had studied during the interwar years was the one he was now facing—the Japanese.

Within one hundred days, Eichelberger would have the opportunity to test his knowledge, experience, and leadership philosophy in some of the toughest fighting of World War II. And he would prevail.

# · 2 ·

# Buna: The Harsh Crucible of Combat

IT HAD BEEN TWENTY YEARS SINCE ROBERT LAWRENCE EICHELBERGER had heard the sound of gunfire under hostile conditions. That was when he was in the frozen environment of Siberia shortly after World War I. His recall to combat would take him to a new environment—the steamy jungles of the South Pacific. He was ready!

On 25 August 1942, after traveling for seven days, the B–24 bomber, which had been assigned to Eichelberger and his staff, landed in Australia. A very tired, rumpled, and disheveled Eichelberger stepped from the aircraft, but he wore the infectious grin that was his trademark. He possessed a magnetic personality and his warmth and sense of humor inspired unstinted loyalty in his subordinates, which would be the key to victory in the South Pacific. He was a grandfather-like figure to his staff. He brought out the best in people by his commonsense and gentlemanly approach to the business of war. At fifty-six years of age, he had not become rigid and set in his ways, probably because he had not served in the trenches of France. He had a flexible and creative intellect, capable of pooling his knowledge and experience in order to develop innovative solutions. He was a man willing to experiment, to try something new, and this trait was admired by his subordinates. In the months to come his intellect, creativity, and leadership style would be sorely tested in the harsh crucible of combat.

## Buna: The Harsh Crucible of Combat

The next morning, after a good night's sleep, Eichelberger met with Lieutenant General Richard Sutherland, MacArthur's chief of staff, whom he had known at Fort Leavenworth. Their greeting that morning was cordial, but their relationship was not destined to stay that way. In personality they were extreme opposites. Sutherland, brilliant, intense, and demanding, lacked the warmth and humanity of Eichelberger. He was cold, aloof, harsh, and abrupt and did not inspire the same confidence in subordinates. Sutherland was also very jealous of his close relationship with MacArthur, and thus did not want any rivals. In the months to come as the tactical situation in the theater deteriorated, Sutherland's personality flaws created serious problems in Australia.

Later that morning Eichelberger's meeting with MacArthur was cordial, but very unsettling. MacArthur, at age sixty-two, was at the height of his power. He was brilliant, creative, and energetic and possessed the physical vigor of a much younger man. MacArthur was feeling pleased to have a corps headquarters to take control of the two American divisions which he had in Australia (the Thirty-second and Forty-first Infantry divisions). This new corps relieved his headquarters of the logistical, administrative, and training responsibilities for the 56,000 men in the two divisions. MacArthur was also glad to see Eichelberger again, since his performance as secretary to the General Staff had been impressive.[1] However, MacArthur's morale at the time of Eichelberger's arrival was not high.

The general strategic situation in the Pacific Theater in August 1942 was bleak. The Japanese war machine seemed to be invincible that summer. It had successfully conquered every objective it had set for itself, and its string of victories was impressive. In December 1941 the Japanese had captured Guam and Wake islands. Also that month they had landed a 100,000-man army, under the command of Lieutenant General Tomoyuki Yamashita, in northern Malaya and a 50,000-man force, commanded by General Masaharu Homma, in the Philippines. Although General Yamashita's army was outnumbered by the British army, commanded by Lieutenant General A. E. Percival, Yamashita skillfully used tanks in the jungle, night infiltrations behind the British lines, and amphibious assaults to drive the British steadily down the peninsula into the fortress at Singapore. On 15 February 1942 General Percival surrendered the British garrison of 70,000 men to the Japanese. This was the single greatest military defeat in the history of the British empire. At a cost of 9,824 casualties, Yamashita had destroyed a British army of 138,700 men.

At the same time British military power in the Pacific was being destroyed, General Homma was having similar success in the Philippines. When General Homma landed in the Philippines on the main island of Luzon on 10 December 1942, he faced General MacArthur's combined American and Filipino ground army of 130,000 men. However, the bulk of this force, 107,000 men, consisted of partly organized and equipped units in the Filipino army. General Homma's objective was to occupy Luzon within fifty days. To thwart Homma, MacArthur planned to withdraw onto the Bataan Peninsula and the island of Corregidor where his firepower would prevent the Japanese from using the port facilities. General MacArthur believed that Luzon would be worthless to the Japanese if the great port at Manila was denied to them. Unfortunately, MacArthur could not hold the Japanese indefinitely without reinforcements and supplies, which were not forthcoming. He was slowly pushed down the Bataan Peninsula. On 11 March 1942, MacArthur departed the Philippines by order of President Franklin D. Roosevelt, and on 6 May General Jonathan Wainwright surrendered to Homma.

After having defeated the Americans and the British, the pace of the Japanese advance quickened. They soon defeated the Dutch forces and seized the Netherlands East Indies. Continuing their advance, the Japanese moved into eastern New Guinea and the Solomon Islands. They hoped, by occupying these forward bases, that they could interdict the sea-lanes between the United States and Australia, thereby cutting Australia's logistical lifeline.[2]

In order for the Japanese to isolate Australia successfully from the logistical support of the United States, they needed to establish a large naval base near the sea-lanes. Port Moresby, the capital of the Papuan Peninsula on the southeastern tip of the island of New Guinea, was the ideal location. The port had a large natural harbor capable of supporting a large fleet and was located directly across the Coral Sea (340 miles) from Australia. Furthermore, from this base the Japanese could stage an invasion of Australia at a later date. In order to continue the momentum of their advance, in May 1942 the Japanese navy tried to take Port Moresby directly by sea. This invasion force collided with elements of the United States Pacific Fleet on 4–8 May in the Battle of the Coral Sea. Although an American aircraft carrier was sunk, which the United States could ill afford to lose, this naval battle was a strategic victory for the United

States Navy because it successfully turned back the Japanese invasion force from Port Moresby.[3]

Despite this setback, the Japanese were still determined to take Port Moresby. This time they decided to take it from the landward side. Thus, on 21 July 1942, the Japanese landed 11,000 troops at Buna and Gona on the northeast coast of Papua. Buna was a small government outpost near a native village, 120 miles north of Port Moresby, and Gona was an Anglican mission, ten miles northwest of Buna. From these the Japanese planned to drive southward across the Papuan Peninsula.[4]

On 26 August 1942, as Eichelberger met with General MacArthur, Major General Tomitaro Horii, the Japanese commander, commenced this southern drive. MacArthur was acutely aware of the consequences of the loss of Port Moresby—the complete isolation of Australia. He also knew that the Japanese army had not yet failed to take any assigned objective and that he had few assets at his disposal. Eichelberger discovered, at that initial meeting, that the situation among the Allies was volatile. The integration of the American and Australian forces was severely hampered by the rivalry between the two armies. Eichelberger had been warned before he left Washington, by Lieutenant General Lesley McNair, that this rivalry had resulted in an "explosive" situation in Australia. General McNair hoped that Eichelberger's tact and personality would help to reduce tensions. When he arrived in Australia, Eichelberger found that many of the Australian generals, who had already been in combat with the British in North Africa, did not think that the Americans would be of much help. Having fought Rommel and the Afrika Corps in the desert, the Australians considered the Americans to be "inexperienced theorists."[5]

The American attitude toward the Australians was just as unfriendly. MacArthur and his staff delighted in pointing out to the Australian high command how poorly the Australian troops had performed in Malaya. While the Australians were rightfully proud of their performance against the Germans, to MacArthur the only enemy was the Japanese. Perhaps it was his own humiliation at the hands of the Japanese that led him to remind the Australians of how badly they had been outclassed in Malaya. MacArthur also believed that the Americans had outperformed the Australians in combat against the Japanese. The Americans had held out for more than five months in the Philippines whereas the British had lasted only six weeks. MacArthur wanted the Australians to put their experiences in the desert behind them and to prepare their soldiers for jungle warfare. Unfortunately, his tactless manner in pointing out the Malayan experience only caused hard feelings and resentment between the Allies. Each army was proud of its own performance thus far in the war and questioned the ability of its ally.[6]

Eichelberger left his initial meeting with MacArthur with the order to establish I Corps headquarters in Rockhampton, Australia, 300 miles north of Brisbane. I Corps was assigned to the Australian First Army under the command of General Sir John Lavarak. General MacArthur had told Eichelberger to pay his "respects to the Australians and then leave them alone. Don't have anything to do with them." Eichelberger found this advice difficult to comply with, since General Lavarak took his command responsibilities very seriously and would not be ignored. The tension and air of suspicion between the Allies resulted in General Lavarak's initial mistrust of Eichelberger. In order to establish his authority, General Lavarak was curt and rude in his correspondence with Eichelberger. Instead of taking offense, Eichelberger always responded in a tactful and cordial manner. In response to official correspondence from Lavarak, Eichelberger wrote personal and friendly letters and always signed them with "warm regards." This friendliness was initially disconcerting to the Australians but, over time, Eichelberger's attitude and high standards of professionalism in training greatly impressed them. He was one of the few senior American officers in Australia who had the foresight to establish a good rapport with the Allies. This relationship with the senior Australian officers later proved a distinct advantage at Buna when I Corps served under Australian command.[7]

Initially, Eichelberger had only a small group of advisers with him in Australia. The rest of his staff arrived by ship on 17 October 1942. The staff officers he brought with him were men of great talent, experience, and vision. Eichelberger did not want or need yes men who would blindly obey his orders. Rather, he valued men who were competent and creative and capable of pooling their knowledge and experience to adapt solutions to fit any given problem.

Eichelberger's chief of staff was Brigadier General Clovis Byers. At forty-two years of age, Byers was one of the youngest corps chiefs of staff in the army. He was vigorous and possessed the stamina to work long hours without rest, and the quality of his work never suffered. He reflected Eichelberger's belief in leadership by example and before the war was over earned the Distinguished Service Cross, Silver Star, and two Bronze Star medals. Eichelberger's intelligence officer was Colonel Gordon Rogers. Rogers, like Byers, was a cavalryman, tough, hard, and aggressive. At forty years of age he also possessed the stamina and vigor to lead men under adverse conditions. Later, in combat, he earned two Distinguished Service Crosses and a Silver Star. Both Rogers and Byers were brilliant soldiers and both retired as lieutenant generals.

Eichelberger had two operations officers with him in Australia. The first, Colonel Charles Martin, was a graduate of the Virginia Military Institute. At forty-six he was one of the oldest men on Eichelberger's staff. A cavalry officer inbued with Eichelberger's style of leadership, he later earned a Distinguished Service Cross and two Silver Stars. He possessed a low-key demeanor and a great deal of common sense. He went on to command a division with distinction in the Pacific. Eichelberger's assistant operations officer in August 1942 was Lieutenant Colonel Frank Bowen. At thirty-three years of age he was young and handsome. Bowen was perhaps the most brilliant and innovative tactician in the army. He was an indefatigable worker and his courage was unquestioned. He earned two Distinguished Service Crosses and four Silver Stars in his career.[8]

Upon arriving in Australia, Eichelberger's principal responsibility was to prepare the I Corps for combat. This entailed supervision of the training programs of the Thirty-second and Forty-first divisions. Both of these divisions were commanded by West Point classmates of Eichelberger. Major General Edwin F. Harding commanded the Thirty-second, a National Guard Division from Wisconsin and Michigan. Harding, one of the most urbane and literate officers in the United States Army, was handsome and in excellent physical condition.[9] General Omar Bradley described Harding as "a man of rare wit, ability, intelligence, and professionalism." Bradley also credited Harding as the man who first influenced him to study his profession.[10] Harding was a personal protégé of General George C. Marshall and had served with Marshall in China and again at Fort Benning. Harding was the man responsible for making *Infantry Journal* into the intellectual and professional forum for the army in the 1930s.[11] The commander of the Forty-first, a National Guard unit from Washington and Oregon, was Major General Horace Fuller. Fuller was a veteran of World War I and was an excellent trainer of troops. He and Eichelberger were very close personal friends and worked well together.[12]

As soon as Eichelberger and his small staff moved to Rockhampton, they conducted training inspections to assess the state of readiness in the Thirty-second and Forty-first divisions. In September 1942 they found that neither of these units was prepared for combat. The Forty-first Division had arrived in Australia on 6 April 1942 with a reputation as "The top ranking National Guard Division and one of the three top Divisions of the whole Army."[13] This assessment of the Forty-first Division was based on its performance in training exercises in the United States. Unfortunately, as early as May 1942 MacArthur discovered that this unit's reputation was highly inflated. At a training inspection his staff found:

> The body of instruction is identical with that given in the U. S. The manner of execution showed little comprehension of the realities of warfare. Regimental, Battalion and junior commands think they are doing a good job. In spite of vigorous representations by the Division Commander and his staff, coupled with a substantial number of changes in command, unit commanders are convinced that they are preparing their units for war. This for the simple reason that they apparently have only the vaguest conception of the realities of combat.[14]

The Forty-first Division had never conducted any maneuvers with live ammunition, and most of the soldiers in the division had never even fired their own weapons.[15] The Japanese, in contrast, were superb in weapon handling; each soldier was an expert with his assigned weapon. In addition, the Japanese soldiers were in excellent physical condition and could endure great hardship. Their doctrine emphasized night-fighting techniques and, by constant training, the Japanese soldier fought best after dark. The Japanese soldiers were also trained for jungle warfare and many had had combat experience in China.[16]

The Thirty-second Division, at the time of Eichelberger's arrival in Australia, was also unprepared for combat. The Thirty-second Division arrived in Adelaide, Australia, on 14 May 1942 without the reputation for efficiency of the Forty-first Division. In January 1942 the Third Army commander, Lieutenant General Walter Krueger, inspected the Thirty-second Division and found that its training was seriously deficient. In order to improve the combat readiness of this troubled division, General Marshall selected Major General Edwin Harding to straighten it out.

The division was under strength by 5,000 men, and many of the officers Harding inherited were over age and under trained. During the coming months the division was to be constantly moved, so very little training was conducted between February and October 1942. When Harding took command of the division in February 1942, it was stationed at Camp Livingston, Louisiana. He first moved the division to Fort Devens, Massachusetts, in preparation for deployment to Europe. The orders were then changed and the division had to be moved across the country to San Francisco for deployment to Australia. Once the division arrived in Australia, it was moved twice as MacArthur's staff tried to determine a good location for it.[17]

During the first week of September 1942, Eichelberger conducted his own inspections of the combat-readiness of both divisions. He found neither prepared for combat and both training programs unrealistic and inadequate. For example, he found that what little training the Thirty-second Division had received was for the defense of Australia, when what they really needed was training for the type of battle they would most likely encounter—jungle warfare. Therefore Eichelberger honestly informed General MacArthur that neither division was "sufficiently trained to meet Japanese veterans on equal terms."[18] Colonel Russell Reeder, an observer from the War Department, concurred with Eichelberger's assessment and stated "that they needed a lot of work."[19]

Eichelberger found that the greatest deficiency in both units was a lack of training in what he called "the simple things, such as scouting and patrolling." A manifestation of this situation was that the Thirty-second Division had conducted only one night problem in twenty months. As soon as Eichelberger had evaluated the combat efficiency of his divisions, he instituted a realistic and demanding training program. He emphasized physical fitness to ensure that his soldiers had the physical stamina to endure in combat. He had his soldiers train in the type of environment that they would most likely have to fight in—the jungle. He demanded that his soldiers train at night and be well trained in the techniques of scouting and patrolling—finding and fighting the enemy in the jungle. He also stressed live-fire exercises, which conditioned the soldiers to the noise and confusion of the battlefield as well as thoroughly familiarizing them with their weapons. Unfortunately, when Eichelberger instituted this rigorous training program in mid-September 1942, two regiments of the Thirty-second Division (126th and 128th regiments) had already deployed forward to New Guinea. Therefore, these two regiments went into battle with a serious handicap.[20]

The Thirty-second Division had hurriedly deployed to New Guinea in September 1942 because General MacArthur had changed his strategy in the theater. The Japanese advance from Buna and Gona, which had started on 26 August, had been stopped on 17 September. General Horii's plan to march 120 miles overland from Buna to Gona to seize Port Moresby looked good on the map, but he had not considered the difficult terrain and climate in New Guinea. One historian later noted that "The Japanese could scarcely have chosen a more dismal place in which to conduct a campaign."[21] Between Buna and Port Moresby lay an almost impenetrable jungle and a great mountain barrier that ran the length of the island, the Owen Stanley Range. Moving through the jungle was an almost impossible task. Between the closely spaced trees was a myriad of thick underbrush, wait-a-minute vines, and tangled roots. There was also thick Kunai grass, which grew over six feet tall and was razor sharp to touch. A man could barely see a few feet ahead. Furthermore, much of the jungle was swampland and several of the swamps were impenetrable. The mountains, more than 13,000 feet high, literally cut the island of New Guinea in half along its east-west axis, leaving only one small native trail that crossed it. It was this trail upon which General Horii attempted to move.

The climate in this region was also debilitating. The temperature averaged 89° F. and the humidity 82 percent, but of even more importance were the health conditions. Malaria, dengue fever, typhus, dysentery, ringworm, scrub typhus, and jungle rot destroyed the combat effectiveness of a unit operating in this region.[22]

After fighting his way out of the jungle and deep into the Owen Stanley, General Horii's drive stalled. His troops were sick and exhausted, and lacked the combat strength to take Port Moresby. Although he needed fresh troops, he did not receive them because the Japanese high command had diverted the bulk of his reinforcements to the battle on Guadalcanal. Therefore, on 18 September General Horii was ordered to pull back to Buna, dig in, and establish a defensive perimeter. Once Guadalcanal was secured and the Americans defeated again, the Japanese high command believed that they could then take Port Moresby.[23]

Douglas MacArthur was a brilliant and daring theater commander. He had a strategic sixth sense, which enabled him to locate and exploit his enemy's vulnerabilities. Ignoring all logistical constraints and the paucity of combat troops in the theater, MacArthur went on the offensive in New Guinea. He decided to seize the initiative and destroy the Japanese beachheads at Buna and Gona. If successful, this would ensure the safety of Port Moresby and secure the sea-lanes between the United States and Australia.

To conduct this offensive, MacArthur planned to use two divisions. The Australian Seventh Division was to attack and destroy the Japanese at Gona while, at the same time, the American Thirty-second Division would eliminate the Japanese garrison at Buna. He selected an Australian officer, Lieutenant General Edmund Herring, to be the field commander for this operation.[24]

Despite the training deficiencies in the Thirty-second Division, MacArthur was gambling that the victory could be won quickly due to the weakened state of the Japanese forces. Although MacArthur's strategic insight was excellent, the Intelligence available to him was faulty. General Charles Willoughby erroneously informed MacArthur that the Japanese garrison at Buna consisted of only 1,500 exhausted survivors of General Horii's overland march on Port Moresby. In reality there were 8,000 Japanese in the area, including 2,500 fresh Japanese troops at Buna. The reinforcements were veterans of China and Malaya and were well trained and confident.[25]

Through October and early November 1942, as Australians and Americans closed in on the Japanese at Gona and Buna, Eichelberger worked diligently to prepare the Forty-first Division for combat. Although he had been unable to condition the Thirty-second Division for the environment they would encounter in New Guinea, the training of the Forty-first Division became an obsession with him. Unfortunately, his desire for information about conditions on New Guinea, in order to update and modify his training program continually, led him into conflict with General Sutherland. In late September Eichelberger made a trip to New Guinea to evaluate the terrain and combat conditions of the region. During this visit he met with General MacArthur and obtained permission to send staff officers to the front in order to observe Japanese tactics. However, by mid-November the situation had changed dramatically. In early November 1942, based on Willoughby's overly optimistic Intelligence reports, Sutherland expected a quick victory at Buna. There is an old military axiom that victory has many fathers, but defeat is an orphan. Therefore Sutherland did not want to share the credit and glory for the first ground victory in the Pacific with anyone else—including the I Corps commander. Thus, when Eichelberger arrived in New Guinea to observe personally conditions at the front, Sutherland ordered him back to Australia. Sutherland curtly informed Eichelberger that his role in the theater was only to train troops and that he was to stay out of New Guinea. Eichelberger, who had recently been promoted to three-star rank, was especially rankled by this treatment from an officer of equal rank. He wrote a close friend that he "had been treated more like a lieutenant than a lieutenant general by the GHQ Chief of Staff."[26] Although Eichelberger possessed a warm and outgoing personality, he was also capable of harboring a grudge. He believed that Sutherland had treated him in an insulting and unprofessional manner and this resulted in a serious deterioration in their relationship in the next six weeks.

It was a slow, tedious, and time-consuming process to move the Australian Seventh Division and American Thirty-second Division from Australia to Port Moresby, New Guinea, and from there across the Owen Stanley mountains to Buna and Gona. Therefore it was not until 14 November 1942 that both units were in position to commence their attacks to destroy the Japanese beachheads at Buna and Gona.

Buna is the most controversial American battle of World War II; historians have derived a variety of interpretations from it. The United States Army has studied this battle in great depth in order to learn of the problems inherent in fighting the first battle of a war. At the Command and General Staff College at Fort Leavenworth, Kansas, army officers between their tenth and fourteenth year of service are sent to study tactics, strategy, staff operations, and leadership. For many years this school has used Buna as a case study in leadership to prepare young officers for the challenges of command in combat. In addition, the army leadership manual for general officers, published in 1986, also uses Buna as a case study in leadership.[27] In order to understand the controversial nature of Buna and the United States Army's continued interest in it, three aspects of the battle must be understood: what went wrong, why, and how the situation was corrected.

At the time MacArthur began the Battle of Buna, he had three serious handicaps to contend with in addition to the Japanese: the inferior quality of his staff, untrained troops, and the seriously strained relationship with the Australians.

An army commander's staff officers are responsible to advise and assist on their specific area of expertise. The word "staff" is supposedly derived from the fact that a commander leans on his staff as he would on a wooden staff or cane.[28] Unfortunately, the criteria for admission to MacArthur's staff was not proven competence and ability. Rather, he surrounded himself with men whose major accomplishment was that they had been with him on Bataan. MacArthur's failure to surround himself with brilliant men of vision had an adverse effect on his operations at Buna.

Charles Willoughby was certainly a great admirer of MacArthur and never challenged him. After the war he wrote a book in which MacArthur was favorably compared to Alexander the Great, Hannibal, and Napoleon. However, his Intelligence reports on the situation found at Buna were grossly inaccurate. Based on Willoughby's erroneous report that there were only 1,500 tired and exhausted Japanese at Buna, General Harding moved in, writing to Eichelberger: "I am confident we can take Buna, and that without too much difficulty . . . I am strong for pushing through to a finish while we have many factors in our favor—complete domination of the air, numbers, and morale. I may be wrong but I have a hunch that the [morale] of the Japs at Buna may not be as high as it has been in previous shows."[29] In reality, the Japanese had a much larger force in the area and they had plenty of time to prepare an elaborate defensive system. The Japanese left flank and rear rested on the ocean, the right flank abutted an unfordable tidal stream, and the front faced an impassable swamp. The only way to reach the Japanese was along four very narrow corridors through the swamp. However, the Japanese had prepared an elaborate network of mutually supporting bunkers, organized in depth along these corridors.[30] The army's official after-action report outlines just how formidable an obstacle these bunkers were:

The Japanese bunkers were almost entirely above ground.
The base of the bunker was a shallow trench, up to 40 feet in length for the large bunkers, and 6 to 10 feet for the smaller.

A framework of columns and beams was set up, the walls were revetted with coconut logs ranging up to 1 1/2 feet in thickness, and a ceiling of two or three courses of such logs was laid on top. Not content with this construction, the enemy reinforced the wall, using steel oil drums and ammunition boxes filled with sand, as well as log piles and rocks. Over all this were piled earth and sand mixed with short logs, coconuts and the like. When the bunker, 7 to 8 feet high, was camouflaged with fast-growing jungle vegetation, it became almost impossible to spot in the tangled underbrush.[31]

On 19 November the Thirty-second Division attacked the Japanese positions confident of an easy victory. They were shocked to find the veteran Japanese soldiers at Buna in almost impregnable positions. The Japanese had more men inside Buna then Harding had attacking it. (Harding had only two of the division's three regiments—the 126th and 128th regiments. The third regiment was under the control of the Australians.) The Japanese soldiers were highly trained, motivated, and skillful at infiltration, camouflage, and placement of machine guns. Most important, they were at their best at night.[32] The Japanese easily blunted the Thirty-second Division's attack. On 21 November General MacArthur, who was at Port Moresby, ordered Harding to "Take Buna today at all costs." Again the Thirty-second Division attacked, and again it was repulsed. In the next ten days, this division suffered 492 battle casualties, but was unable to make a single penetration of the enemy line.[33]

MacArthur was naturally disappointed that his first offensive of the war was not progressing as he had planned; however, he did not go to the front to inspect the situation for himself. MacArthur believed that more troops at the front might be a solution. Therefore he recommended to the Australians, on 25 November, that the Forty-first Division be brought to New Guinea to reinforce the Thirty-second Division. The Australian commander countered with the proposal that Australian troops be brought over instead because they could be counted on to fight. The Australians were openly challenging the spirit and fighting ability of the Americans—another example of the rivalry between the Allies. The Thirty-second Division's stalemate at Buna gave the Australians an opportunity to get even with MacArthur for his numerous comments about their poor showing in Malaya. Instead of helping each other, the Allies were gloating over their partner's difficulties.[34]

Furthermore, Port Moresby was rampant with rumors about the breakdown in discipline and leadership at the front. While many of the armchair warriors, safe and secure in Port Moresby, pointed out the deficiencies of the Thirty-second Division, General Harding was getting very little assistance. MacArthur, appalled by the rumors and the idle gossip in Port Moresby, sent two inspection teams from his G–3 Operations office to the front to investigate. On 27 November they reported to MacArthur that the soldiers were not fighting and "preferred to stand off and attempt to kill at a distance with their rifles or have aircraft, mortars, or artillery do the job for them."[35] They also criticized General Harding for the location of command post, which they felt was too far from the front. However, this report, typical of the poor quality produced by MacArthur's staff, never got to the crux of the problem. Harding did not have the weapons to reduce the Japanese bunker network. To do this he needed artillery and tanks, which were not forthcoming because General Kenney, believing that the "artillery in this theater flies," had convinced MacArthur that it was not needed. Unfortunately, the Air Force was incapable of locating and destroying the bunkers in the jungle. The Australians, who had tanks, were in competition with the Americans and therefore would not share them.[36]

In addition to lacking tanks and artillery, General Harding had several other problems during his first two weeks in combat. The fact that his soldiers were not prepared for combat cannot be overemphasized. They were trained only for frontal attacks on the bunkers, and these attacks were suicidal. Since they could not move at night, night operations to attack the bunkers were out of the question. Infiltration and night patrolling to find and destroy the bunkers might have worked, but Harding thought that the cost in human lives would be prohibitive.[37] Harding found that even dawn attacks were impossible because his men got lost just trying to move into their attack positions at night. Furthermore, since they were the first American army unit deployed into a jungle environment, they had to learn this type of warfare by experience.

Harding was also having problems with the terrain, morale, and his staff. Movement in the jungle, even in daylight, was arduous. The soldiers were demoralized because they were suffering casualties, yet were unable to see the enemy. Sickness was also taking its toll: for every two men wounded, five were out of action due to malaria or some other disease.[38] The staff work in the Thirty-second Division also caused problems for General Harding. The pressure and heavy pace of combat exacerbated the planning deficiencies within the division. The troops were short on food and ammunition, and this was partly due to poor staff work.[39]

The biggest problem that Harding had to contend with was the breakdown in discipline and the development of a siege mentality. This is exemplified by examining an article written by a first sergeant in one of the division's infantry companies. The first sergeant wrote: "Company E stayed in that spot for most of ten days fighting a battle of nerves." The first sergeant obviously did not understand that the division's mission was to conquer Buna, not to try to lay siege to the Japanese and starve them out. He then went on to say, "They improved their foxholes whenever they had a chance, digging with helmets and bayonets and empty ration cans, but mostly with their hands." This is another example of the breakdown in discipline in the Thirty-second Division. Every soldier was issued an entrenching tool, but the soldiers had thrown them away. The first sergeant then wrote, "The soldiers were hungry, but that was nothing new for them." However, the reason the soldiers were hungry was that the staff had failed adequately to requisition and distribute rations.[40]

On 30 November General Sutherland inspected conditions at the front. After a brief visit he recommended that Harding relieve both of his regimental commanders—Colonels J. Tracey Hale and John Mott. Hale was a very friendly and personable lawyer from Milwaukee. He had had combat experience in World War I and was a long-time National Guard officer. Unfortunately, he lacked the tactical expertise and physical stamina for an extended campaign in the jungle. His greatest problem, however, was his inability to delegate responsibility, and he "was worn down to a frazzle" as he tried to do everything himself. Since he was the last National Guard officer in charge of a regiment in the Thirty-second Division, Harding hesitated to relieve him.[41]

Colonel Mott was a forty-five-year-old officer with a difficult and trying disposition. His sarcastic manner caused him to make enemies of many people with whom he had contact. Although he was intelligent and had received an M.B.A. from Harvard in 1941, he had not attended either the Command and General Staff College or the

Army War College. In the jungle he sorely needed the tactical experience and knowledge that these schools would have provided.[42]

Harding, a gentleman with a strict sense of honor and integrity, was intensely loyal to his subordinates. Believing that they had worked enthusiastically for him, he refused to act upon General Sutherland's suggestion that they be replaced. Unfortunately, Harding's loyalty was misplaced. The division would have been better off with more tactically experienced and dynamic regimental commanders.

In response to Harding's lack of action, Sutherland, who was always willing to make the tough decisions, returned to Port Moresby to recommend that MacArthur relieve Harding. MacArthur's legendary poise and confidence were shaken on the evening of 30 November 1942. He believed that he had personally failed in the Philippines, and now his first offensive of the war also seemed doomed to a similar fate. The Australians took a perverse delight in his problems and, in his mind, so did many of his enemies back in Washington. MacArthur, realizing that the Forty-first Division lacked the training and fighting spirit to change seriously the situation at the front, knew that the only solution was to send in a dynamic and inspirational leader. He therefore had Eichelberger flown in from Australia.[43]

When Eichelberger stepped onto the veranda of MacArthur's headquarters on 30 November, he was completely ignorant of the bleak tactical situation on Buna. Sutherland had kicked Eichelberger off New Guinea two weeks earlier when the victory seemed a foregone conclusion. Due to censorship, Eichelberger had not heard that the Thirty-second Division had encountered any difficulties. Therefore Eichelberger did not know the reasons for the abrupt summons and the grim faces that greeted him. Only the feisty General Kenney smiled at Eichelberger with warmth and friendship. Generals Willoughby and Sutherland were cold and aloof as they stood in the background. MacArthur, holding center stage, was animated, but visibly shaken. Eichelberger was completely unprepared for the order he received. MacArthur said:

> Bob, I'm putting you in command at Buna. Relieve Harding.
> I am sending you in, Bob, and I want you to remove all
> officers who won't fight. Relieve Regimental and Battalion
> commanders; if necessary, put Sergeants in charge of
> Battalions and Corporals in charge of companies—anyone

who will fight. Time is of the essence; the Japs may land reinforcements any night . . . I want you to take Buna, or not come back alive.[44]

That evening Eichelberger puzzled over that order. Normally a commander is given an operations order, instructions that clearly state "the situation, the mission, the plan of action, and those details that insure the coordinated, efficient and effective execution necessary to obtain maximal performance from the command."[45] But Eichelberger had received no information about Buna, just an emotional command to take Buna or "not come back alive."

The next morning, before Eichelberger boarded the aircraft that would fly him to Buna, he again met with General MacArthur, who by now was more in control of himself and somewhat more self-assured. He told Eichelberger that, when Buna was taken, he would award him the Distinguished Service Cross, recommend him for a high British Decoration, and release his name to the press. Eichelberger then departed for Buna.[46]

In the next thirty-two days, Eichelberger was involved in the most brutal battle of World War II. His professional development as a combat commander would be honed in this harsh crucible of combat. The casualties suffered because of the unpreparedness of the officers and men of the Thirty-second Division would result in his ruthless avocation of a realistic training program. And his battle tactics would be forever influenced by Buna.[47]

Eichelberger, and a small staff of trusted officers, landed at Buna at 1100 hours on 1 December. His first directive was to General Herring, informing him that he was anxious to cooperate with the Australians. Although this may seem a small and insignificant action, it prompted General Herring to dispatch his chief of staff, Brigadier R. Hopkins, to Buna, to confer with Eichelberger. Hopkins told Eichelberger that Herring had been touched by his message and then asked him to send all requests for air support through the Australian New Guinea Force headquarters. Hopkins stated that this had not been done before, but General Harding, who was present, vehemently denied this allegation. Eichelberger stepped in and cut off this argument, promising Hopkins that he would comply with the Australians' request. Thus, in his first few hours at the front, Eichelberger acknowledged his subordinate position to General Herring, despite their equal rank, and established a rapport with the

Australians. Eichelberger then sat in on a number of briefings by Harding's staff in order to become acquainted with the tactical situation at the front.[48]

The terrain at Buna was a problem. The huge, impassable swamp that lay before the Japanese positions forced Harding to establish two separate and distinct fronts, rather than a single, coordinated front. Colonel Mott commanded the left, or Urbana, front (named after Eichelberger's hometown). Colonel Hale commanded the right, or Warren, front (Harding's home county in Ohio).[49]

On the morning of 2 December, Eichelberger directed two of his staff officers, Colonel Clarence Martin and Colonel Gordon Rogers, to inspect conditions on the right flank (Warren front) while he visited the left flank (Urbana front). General MacArthur, a man Eichelberger admired, had been visibly shaken by conditions at Buna, and he had ordered Eichelberger to relieve Harding. Eichelberger had known Harding for thirty-seven years. Harding had an excellent reputation in the army, and Eichelberger knew that General George C. Marshall, the chief of staff, considered him a protégé. Additionally, Harding was a man of great personal courage and had already been recommended by his men for a Silver Star. Eichelberger decided that he would see for himself what the situation was like at the front and then decide what to do about Harding.[50]

Before Eichelberger even got to the front line on the left flank, he discovered a serious morale problem. He came upon an informal rest area with more than a hundred men lounging around. There was no one in charge; the men had been sent there by their platoon leaders or sergeants, as individuals, for a rest. When questioned by Eichelberger, the men did not know how long they would be there. Unfortunately this was not an isolated incident. Colonel Rogers, on the right flank, discovered that of the 2,000 infantrymen who were supposed to be manning foxholes on the front line, only 150 were actually there. The other 1,850 infantrymen were scattered all over the place. Rogers believed that "it would have been impossible to organize and employ them." This is a strong indicator that the chain of command had broken down. The commanders did not know where their men were and, in reality, the situation was so far out of control that the Thirty-second Division was not an effective fighting force. Harding's regimental commanders had indeed let him down.[51]

Eichelberger was also shocked at the ineptness and confusion of those few troops actually manning the frontline positions. There was no unit cohesion. Platoons, companies, and battalions did not have their own clearly designated sector of responsibility on the line. Instead, the few troops in the foxholes were from various different units and "scrambled like eggs." Eichelberger found this lack of even rudimentary competence especially disheartening.[52]

Eichelberger and his staff were most astounded and depressed by the physical appearance of the soldiers on both fronts. These men had long, shaggy beards and were incredibly dirty. It was obvious that no system of sanitation was enforced. More important, the men were gaunt and skeletal in appearance. Major Roger Egeberg, one of MacArthur's physicians, said these men looked like "Christ off the Cross." The harsh reality was that these American soldiers were literally starving to death at the front. They had not had a hot meal in ten days and they were existing on two cans of combat rations per day, or 1,800 calories. This was not enough food to exist on, much less to conduct strenuous offensive operations.

That evening Eichelberger discovered the reasons for this sorry state of affairs. Harding's supply officer was simply not capable of handling the logistical requirements of an independent command. General Kenney's Air Force was flying in plenty of food, which was piled high in the airfield, but the supply officer did not know how much and did not have an efficient system for delivering the food to the units. The division supply officer should have been relieved, but Harding did not do this. Another reason for the abominable appearance of the American soldiers was the absence of vigorous leadership. The men had thrown away their packs with food and ammunition because they were too heavy. The uniforms of the American soldiers were in rags, but the Aboriginals in New Guinea were wearing new American field uniforms, which they had found in these packs.[53]

The lack of food, formidable Japanese opposition, and jungle environment had a serious effect on the over-aged and under-trained junior officers and sergeants. These junior leaders, instead of becoming a source of inspiration for their soldiers, tended to commiserate with them, leading many to think that if the division waited long enough someone else would be sent in to finish the job. Eichelberger's staff noticed that many of the officers were at the command posts talking to their soldiers in nervous, hushed tones. This attitude had resulted in a complete breakdown in military courtesy at the front. The enlisted men treated their officers as peers. They spoke to them from a reclining or sitting position, even in the rear areas. One of the I Corps officers summed it up by saying, "Saluting was about as rare as snow in Papua."[54]

That evening a very tired and concerned Eichelberger met with his own staff and tried to assess what they had observed during the day. Despite his thirty-three years in the army, and his constant study of military history at West Point, the Command and Staff College, and the Army War College, Eichelberger could not have envisioned taking command under more desperate conditions. The Japanese were in excellent positions and their use of the jungle terrain was admirable. After the punishment they had inflicted on the Americans, their morale was naturally very high. The American situation, on the other hand, was a nightmare. The Americans were physically exhausted from lack of food and disease (50 percent of the division would eventually get malaria). They were mentally depressed because of their lack of preparation, inept Intelligence, and formidable opposition. Furthermore, Harding did not have the vigorous and inspirational regimental commanders capable of leading the Americans to victory.

Eichelberger's first solution to the problems at Buna was to recommend to Harding that he relieve both his regimental commanders. He had on his own staff several tough, demanding, and highly competent colonels, capable of revitalizing the chain of command at the front, and he was offering these men to Harding. However, Harding refused to consider the relief of his subordinates. This put Eichelberger in a difficult position. He was under orders from MacArthur to relieve Harding, a task Eichelberger did not relish. He had soldiered for almost four decades with Harding, and he empathized with the latter's situation. He knew many of Harding's problems were not of his own making, that he suffered from poor planning and Intelligence from MacArthur's staff, and the biting rivalry between MacArthur and the Australians. Yet Harding had committed the cardinal sin of letting his chain of command deteriorate, to the detriment of the American soldier. Harding had to go!

Shortly before midnight that evening, Eichelberger relieved Harding (who took the news stoically) and both his regimental commanders. Eichelberger moved with alacrity on their replacements.[55] He replaced Harding with Brigadier General Albert Waldron, Harding's artillery commander, a short, slim officer described as having an aggressive and pugnacious personality. The new division commander had been a West Point classmate of Eisenhower and Bradley and had served in Mexico and France under General Pershing. Eichelberger was confident Waldron could do the job. To give him maximum support, Eichelberger named new regimental commanders. He put Colonel Clarence Martin, a World War I combat veteran, in charge of the Warren front, and Colonel John Grose, another World War I veteran, in command of the Urbana front. Grose had been I Corps's inspector general.[56]

In the next forty-eight hours, Eichelberger's performance as a leader, manager, and warrior was of the calibre that legends are made of. His first order, based on common sense, was to call a two-day halt in the fighting and to allow his new regimental commanders time to unscramble their units and establish a new and functioning chain of command. Also this halt gave the individual soldiers time to rest and catch up on their sleep when not on duty, without the tension of battle. On 3 December he provided the troops with their first hot meal in more than ten days. Eichelberger believed that hot food, warmed stomachs, and a good night's rest were great morale builders.

Eichelberger's most serious problem was to revitalize the chain of command and to give the infantrymen confidence in themselves and in their leaders. He had to make them into winners who believed that they could defeat the Japanese. From his days in Panama, he realized that jungle warfare was different and more demanding than normal operations. In the jungle, small clusters of men carried the attack without the support usually associated with open terrain. With aggressive leadership at the squad (ten men) and platoon (thirty men) levels, Eichelberger was convinced the Japanese could be defeated.[57]

To revitalize the Warren force chain of command, Colonel Martin called a meeting of all his officers, during which he attempted to instill pride, discipline, and aggressiveness in his junior leaders. At this meeting he insisted that they stop commiserating in front of their men. He also told them that conquering Buna was their mission and theirs alone. He told them there were only two ways off the island of New Guinea: as the conquerors of Buna or as dead men. Colonel Martin also informed them he would hold them personally responsible for supervising and inspecting the appearance and equipment of their men.[58]

While this was going on, Eichelberger strengthened the staff of the Thirty-second Division. He brought in qualified officers from Australia and assigned them to the Thirty-second Division's staff. This improved the staff's efficiency, especially in the areas of supply and planning. General Herring, Eichelberger's Australian superior, came over to Buna on 3 December to inspect things. Herring was greatly impressed with Eichelberger, both as a soldier and as a leader. This attitude would increase after he saw the results of Eichelberger's first thrust into the Japanese stronghold.

Eichelberger's first attack on Buna was launched on the morning of 5 December by well-rested and well-fed soldiers. The logistical support was adequate. The forces had been reorganized under effective chains of command and the soldiers were fighting with an intensity that had not previously been displayed. So far Eichelberger had shown outstanding organizational and administrative skill in sorting out the mess he had inherited on 2 December. On 5 December he set the example for personal courage against the Japanese, which all others sought to emulate that day.

At 1030 hours Eichelberger sent a coordinated attack against the Japanese from both flanks, with all his most trusted staff officers leading to ensure that the soldiers at every level of command understood what was expected of them. The attack did not start auspiciously. On the right flank the Americans were unable to break through the Japanese perimeter, and on the left flank they were stopped initially. However, Eichelberger was present on the left flank and his leadership provided the margin for victory. He boldly walked among the infantrymen wearing the three silver stars of his rank, so that every private would see that he was sharing their danger. The young and inexperienced company commanders were surprised and impressed that the general was in the thick of the fighting with them. Eichelberger believed his presence would rally the troops and also give him the best vantage point to assess the battle. General Waldron was wounded in the shoulder while leading his men against the bunkers of Buna Village, and General Eichelberger's aide, Captain Daniel Edwards, was severely wounded in the thigh while advancing against the enemy with Eichelberger. Edwards was a short, tough North Carolinian who had boxed at Duke University and obtained a law degree from Harvard. He would eventually rejoin Eichelberger.

Eichelberger's personal leadership paid off in success on the left flank that day. A platoon of G Company, 126th Infantry Regiment, destroyed a number of bunkers and drove a wedge to the sea between Buna Mission and Buna Village. This breakthrough isolated and cut off Buna Village from the Japanese main body and it was the first victory for the Thirty-second Division in combat.[59] The victory was important to Eichelberger for three reasons: first, it gave him credibility in his demands for support from his superiors; second, it gained for him the respect and cooperation of the Australians; third, his soldiers gained a new confidence in their own abilities.

Harding knew Buna could not be taken without tanks. However, MacArthur's rift with the Australians and the general ineptitude of Harding's staff meant he would never get the support he needed. However, Eichelberger's initial victory at Buna changed all that and his request for more troops and flame-throwers was granted. Even Herring was impressed with what Eichelberger had accomplished in so short a time. So Eichelberger's request for seven tanks was readily fulfilled by the Australians. The Aussies also sent a battalion of troops under one of their best commanders, Brigadier George F. Wooten. Eichelberger also used his enhanced rapport with the Australians and MacArthur's staff to improve his supply situation at Buna. He built up a stockpile of rations, so that his men could continue to receive hot meals, as well as vitamins, salt tablets, and chlorine pills.[60]

In the brutal, savage fighting on 5 December, the soldiers earned a new respect and confidence in their own abilities. This new confidence, plus the influx of another infantry regiment, the knowledge that the Australians were sending tanks, the improved supply situation, and the revitalized chain of command, dramatically improved the morale and combat effectiveness of the Thirty-second Division.[61]

Although Eichelberger had performed a minor miracle in his first five days at the front, the battle was far from over. He could not afford to let the victory on 5 December go to his head. He realistically assessed what had gone right and what had gone wrong during the battle. On the positive side, his leadership philosophy, which emphasized sharing hardships and dangers with his men, had proved highly successful. On the negative side, the inadequate training of the soldiers and the frontal assaults on the bunkers had resulted in high casualties. Eichelberger realized that he could not afford many more victories like that of 5 December. He knew he had to devise a new method of destroying the Japanese bunkers.

Eichelberger decided that the way to accomplish his task—finding the Japanese bunkers in the jungle and then destroying them at a minimum cost in American lives—was for each company to send out a small patrol at night in front of its position. The patrol would surreptitiously move through the enemy territory until it discovered a Japanese bunker, call in mortar fire, then move up and destroy the bunker. This was a slow process but very effective. The major problem with implementing this tactic was the poor state of training in the Thirty-second Division. Movement through the jungle in daylight was difficult; for troops that had never had any night training, it would have seemed impossible. But Eichelberger was an adaptable sort. He conducted an on-the-job training program. Each night, every company sent out a patrol, which filled out a report on what it saw. This report was then forwarded to division headquarters. Eichelberger personally reviewed so many of these reports that he quipped, "I don't know whether or not I am a good general, but sure as hell I am one fine platoon leader."[62]

Eichelberger successfully utilized this infiltration technique, from 6–14 December, to tighten the noose on Buna Village. His persistence was rewarded on 14 December when the village fell. That night General MacArthur, overcome by joy, sent this message to Eichelberger: "My heartiest congratulations. Under your magnificent leadership the 32nd Division is coming into its own. It was well done Bob."[63]

Although the American forces had secured their initial objective and had significantly narrowed the ground held by the Japanese, the main objective, Buna Mission, was still in Japanese hands. The fighting at Buna was still very much in doubt, and Eichelberger had to deal with a myriad of problems. First, the cumulative impact of disease, battle casualties, and prolonged exposure to combat was sapping the morale of the division. At the same time he had to contend with General MacArthur's demands and the erroneous reports of the Bataan Gang.

By 15 December there was a shortage of men in the rifle companies. The leadership in some units also began to unravel, because many officers and sergeants lacked the physical stamina and mental toughness required for prolonged combat. That day, when Eichelberger visited the front, he found the troops tired and unaggressive. They didn't know where the Japanese positions were and they didn't want to know. One soldier told Eichelberger not to fire, because he might get shot at. Eichelberger's response was to fire his weapon, but the Japanese did not answer. Eichelberger told General Sutherland that evening, "If I have to arm the headquarters clerks and sergeants to get a little leadership, I am going to do it . . . I intend to put all the fight I can into this crowd that they will take and then add some more."[64]

Eichelberger took several dramatic steps and again shook up the leadership at the front by relieving the weakest battalion commanders. He replaced these men with young, vigorous, and dynamic soldiers. One of these new battalion commanders was Captain Gordon Clarkson, who, at twenty-six, was only four years out of West Point. Clarkson had been a brand-new lieutenant in the Thirtieth Infantry when Eichelberger had been the regimental commander. Eichelberger knew that he was tough, honest, and fair. Clarkson, who became dissatisfied with his training assignment in the United States, begged Eichelberger to get him a combat assignment. He did. Clarkson never let Eichelberger down and always accomplished the tough missions. He finished this campaign as a twenty-six-year-old lieutenant colonel with the Distinguished Service Cross.[65]

Unfortunately, Eichelberger had other problems to contend with besides the Japanese at Buna. General MacArthur was not satisfied with the pace of the Thirty-second Division's advance. He continually pressed Eichelberger to attack quickly. His memos stated, "Time is fleeting and our dangers increase with its passage . . . Remember that your mission is to take Buna . . . It can only be done in battle and sooner or later this battle must be engaged . . . Time is working desperately against us."[66]

MacArthur did not understand jungle warfare. He had received his combat experience in the trenches in World War I. During that war he had displayed great personal gallantry and developed an outstanding reputation for leadership. But his mental image of war was also crystallized during this conflict. He viewed battles as being fought and won by large numbers of men massed against a small portion of the enemy line. He wrote Eichelberger: "Your problem is to apply your full power on your front line rather than limit it to two or three companies. Where you have a company of your firing line, you should have a Battalion; and where you have a Battalion, you should have a Regiment. And your attacks, instead of being made by two or three hundred rifles, should be made by two or three thousand."[67] MacArthur did not realize that in the jungle Eichelberger had no place to mass 3,000 riflemen. Also, MacArthur's statement is based on the assumption that each battalion had about 700 men in it. However, at this point in the battle, the battalions had been reduced to less than 180 men each.

MacArthur's impression of conditions at the front was also hindered by the inaccurate reports of his staff. On several occasions he sent Generals Willoughby and Sutherland to observe the fighting at the front. These two staff officers never explained to MacArthur the difficulty of the operations at Buna. An example of this inaccurate reporting took place on 28 December, when General Sutherland visited the front. The soldiers of the Thirty-second were suffering heavy casualties trying to reduce an elaborate network of eighteen bunkers at a position know as "the bunker." General Sutherland climbed a tree, at some distance from the triangle, and declared these defensive positions as "hasty fortifications." (Hasty fortifications are the type of foxhole that one man with a shovel could prepare in a short period of time.) With this type of reporting from his staff, it is no wonder that MacArthur did not appreciate Eichelberger's problems at Buna.[68]

In the period 16 December 1942–2 January 1943, Eichelberger's physical stamina and leadership were tested further. General Clovis Byers, who had taken command of the Thirty-second Division after General Waldron was wounded, was himself wounded on 16 December. This left Eichelberger as the only general officer at the front, so he personally took command of the Thirty-second Division for the remainder of the fighting at Buna.

During this period Eichelberger was a human dynamo. He coordinated with the Australians and MacArthur, commanded the division, and personally visited the men at the front. He utilized every leadership technique that he could muster to motivate his men to attack. Eichelberger's habit was to move among the men and pass out cigarettes, while he praised and flattered them. When he came upon a soldier who had done well, Eichelberger was prompt to decorate him. But if these positive techniques did not work, Eichelberger knew how to be tough. He embarrassed one battalion into conducting an attack by telling them that MacArthur was ashamed of their performance. He told General Sutherland "Somebody has got to plead for my immortal soul because strange words of profanity have rolled out of my face that I never knew I understood." And when even this technique didn't work, he threatened to execute any officer who didn't obey his order to place snipers in the trees.[69]

During this period the Thirty-second Division methodically and relentlessly attacked the Japanese. Captured Japanese diaries indicated that the enemy had developed a new and grudging respect for the Thirty-second Division. On 5 December a Japanese soldier wrote: "The enemy has received almost no training, even though we fire a shot they present a large portion of their body and look around. Their movements are very slow. At that rate they can't even make a night attack."[70] By two weeks later, after Eichelberger had devised innovative tactics, enforced patrolling, revamped the chain of command, and displayed unparalleled inspirational leadership, a Japanese soldier wrote with despair:

> With the dawn the enemy starts shooting all over. All I can
> do is shed tears of resentment. Now we are waiting only for
> death. The news that reinforcement had come turned out to
> be a rumor. All day we stay in the bunkers. We are filled
> with vexation. Comrades are you going to stand by and watch
> us die? Even the invincible Imperial Army is at a loss.[71]

While the Japanese morale was cracking, Eichelberger continued to batter through their defenses. His drive and tenacity were rewarded on 2 January when his troops captured Buna Mission. It had taken him just thirty-two days to take Buna.

Eichelberger did not have any time to savor this victory. Although he had won the battle, the campaign was not yet over. There were still 6,000 Japanese on the Papuan Peninsula. The bulk of this force was dug in around Sanananda, where the Australians had been stymied by their defensive positions for several weeks. On 8 January MacArthur announced to the world that the Papuan campaign was over, except for "mopping up," and returned to Australia. General Herring then moved back to Port Moresby to command all operations on New Guinea. The Australian general's admiration for Eichelberger was such that he appointed him field commander at Sanananda. This entailed command of a corps comprised of both

Australian and American units. This was the first time in the war that the Australians placed their troops under the tactical command of an American officer.

The command was quite a surprise for Eichelberger. For thirty-two days he had pushed himself to his physical limit. He had made every soldier in the division give more than they thought they were capable of. He had conquered a previously unbeaten foe with a reputation for invincibility. Then he was given a new command and another tough mission. Eichelberger was emotionally drained after Buna. He had a warm and close relationship with his staff, three of whom had been wounded. Eichelberger constantly worried about Clovis Byers, Gordon Rogers, and Dan Edwards. Eichelberger always set the example for everyone else to emulate. He accepted the task of capturing Sanananda. However, this campaign was different. Eichelberger was like a sword, and the fire that had forged the steel in his soul was Buna. Never again in his career would Eichelberger have to fight a battle with as many handicaps as at Buna. Although the Australians anticipated that the Sanananda campaign would last several months, it took Eichelberger only ten days to capture it and secure Papua.[72]

One of the major reasons for this success was the employment of the Forty-first Division. This unit had benefited from all the lessons learned at Buna without having to pay the high cost in casualties. Throughout the toughest fighting at Buna, Eichelberger still found time to send letters to General Fuller describing the problems he encountered and the solutions that were successful. General Fuller and the Forty-first Division had four extra months to prepare for combat, and in this period Eichelberger had insisted that they concentrate on night patrolling, physical fitness, jungle training, and exercises in which units maneuvered firing live ammunition. His foresight was rewarded by the outstanding performance of this unit in combat.[73]

With the fall of Sanananda, Eichelberger returned to Australia. He had expected to return to the adulation and admiration of MacArthur and his staff. In this he was bitterly disappointed. He had risked his life daily, seen close subordinates seriously wounded, and pulled MacArthur's chestnuts out of the fire. He had salvaged MacArthur's first offensive of the war and commenced his legend as a military genius. However, Eichelberger was not prepared for his reward. He did receive a Distinguished Service Cross; but instead of writing him an individual citation, MacArthur put his name on a list with ten other generals, most of whom had never heard a bullet fired in anger. What hurt Eichelberger most about this decoration was that the soldiers at Buna had recommended him for the Congressional Medal of Honor. General George C. Marshall, after reviewing the affidavits, was prepared to approve it, when without explanation MacArthur vetoed it. Eichelberger never understood why this was done and MacArthur would not discuss it. Eichelberger was made an Honorary Knight of the Military Division of the most excellent order of the British Empire and his name was released to the press on 9 January 1943.

Eichelberger soon found this last reward more trouble than it was worth. In February and March 1943 Eichelberger's name and picture appeared in many prominent newspapers and magazines in the United States. He was very popular with the reporters in Australia and he received almost as much publicity as MacArthur. MacArthur deeply resented this and summoned Eichelberger to his office for a brief meeting. MacArthur said, "Do you realize I could reduce you to the grade of colonel tomorrow and send you home?" Eichelberger responded, "Of course you could." MacArthur replied, "Well, I won't do it." However, Eichelberger had received the message: if he wanted a career he had better avoid publicity.[74]

Eichelberger and MacArthur had an enigmatic relationship. Although MacArthur did not want a rival for publicity in the Southwest Pacific, he did want a fireman capable of handling the most difficult tactical operations. MacArthur and his staff, after studying the battle in detail in 1943, realized that Eichelberger was a peerless field commander. They knew that they needed him in the theater, in case something ever went wrong again. He had their respect, but he wasn't liked. MacArthur had to be careful that Eichelberger's exploits didn't overshadow him, and the Bataan Gang envied his ability.

Buna had changed Eichelberger. He still treated his staff as if they were members of his own family and was a grandfather-like figure to his troops. Outwardly he was warm and friendly to the Australians and to MacArthur's staff. He still wore a smile and his blue eyes twinkled, but now something simmered just below the surface of those blue pools. At Buna his eyes had burned with intensity and determination. There he had been the quintessential warrior on the battlefield; he had won despite obstacles, bad luck, and the incompetence of others. When he came back he was determined never to be in that situation again. The next time it would be the Japanese who would have to worry about facing the veteran American soldiers. Next time, they would know fear.

At Buna, Eichelberger had learned three important lessons that would give him the edge in the future. First, he learned the importance of a realistic training program. Many American soldiers had died at Buna because they had not been prepared for battle. So Eichelberger established a harsh and demanding training program in Australia. This program emphasized physical conditioning, night patrolling, and constant maneuvering in the jungle. He emphasized squad, platoon, company, and battalion exercises where everyone fired their weapons, including artillery. Eichelberger also stressed mental conditioning, which prepared his men for combat. The next time he went into battle, he was determined to have tough, fit, and competent soldiers under his command.

Second, Eichelberger learned about tactics at Buna. He would never again make a frontal attack if he could avoid it, nor would he allow soldiers to probe enemy lines slowly or develop a siege mentality. In the future, speed would be the hallmark of his operations. He would go in fast, rupture the enemy's offenses, and keep on going. He would never again allow himself to be stuck in a battle of attrition, like that at Buna. He had studied the Japanese operations and believed the attacks from the flank and rear provided the best opportunity for success. Therefore these were the tactics he would use.

Third, Buna consolidated Eichelberger's philosophy of leadership. In the hell of combat at Buna, the margin between victory and defeat had been his style of leadership. Eichelberger lived at the front and shared the dangers and discomforts with his men. He always went to the most critical point on the battlefield so that he was privy to the facts needed to make fast decisions. He believed in leadership by example, and he had inspired his troops to superhuman efforts. In the future he would promote and support those commanders with this philosophy while ruthlessly weeding out those who did not.

Eichelberger had learned these lessons at Buna while commanding only a single division. He soon would head an army corps, and he would repay the Japanese many times over for the lessons they taught him at Buna.

# · 3 ·

# Buna Avenged and Another Fire

On 24 January 1943, just two days after the completion of the Sanananda campaign, Eichelberger turned over command of all American forces in northern New Guinea to his friend Major General Horace Fuller. Eichelberger trusted Fuller, a short, chain-smoking man who had trained the Forty-first Division to a razor's edge. The division had performed brilliantly in the recent campaign.

A hot, exhausted, and much thinner Eichelberger boarded an airplane for the flight back to Australia. He was accompanied by his corps staff who had survived the campaign. During the flight he mused over the events of the past two months. The fighting had been difficult and he was justifiably proud of his hard-won victories at Buna and Sanananda. He realized that MacArthur and his staff did not appreciate the problems he had encountered, but he resolved to put that behind him. He looked forward to meeting with the reporters waiting to interview him, since MacArthur had reluctantly acknowledged his role in the Buna victory.

Eichelberger arrived at Rockhampton, Australia, to a hero's welcome. The Australian high command, which held Eichelberger in the highest esteem, laid out the red carpet. The Australian and American press corps immediately interviewed him and were enamored of his engaging personality.

Over the next two weeks Eichelberger was constantly surrounded by reporters. He was a personable hero, and his picture appeared on the cover of *Life* magazine and in countless newspapers worldwide. Eichelberger, naturally, reveled in the media attention. However, he did not consider MacArthur's chagrin at all this exposure.[1]

Because of his successes against the Japanese and his enormous popularity with the press, Eichelberger expected to command the next operation. He soon discovered that General MacArthur had brought in a new army commander—Lieutenant General Walter Krueger—to control future ground operations. Eichelberger had hoped that his performance at Buna would result in his elevation to army commander, and he was surprised and disappointed by this turn of events. Eichelberger was bluntly informed by General Krueger that all the operations conducted in the theater in 1943 would be division-sized or smaller, making Eichelberger's sole responsibility the training of new divisions in Australia.[2]

Eichelberger also was surprised by the attitude of MacArthur's staff. General Clyde D. Eddleman, the G–3 (operations officer) of the new Sixth Army, later said he had been told by MacArthur's staff that Eichelberger had been slow in taking Buna. The only explanation for the comment was either jealousy over Eichelberger's fame and publicity or guilt over their own errors in this campaign. For whatever reason, MacArthur's staff did their best to ignore Eichelberger's accomplishments at Buna. As late as 1966 Brigadier General Jack Sverdrup, MacArthur's engineer officer, strongly protested the inclusion of Buna as one of the campaigns etched in granite on the new MacArthur Barracks at West Point. However, by 1966 the truth of Eichelberger's actions was known throughout the army and Buna was memorialized on MacArthur Barracks.[3]

During the first few months of 1942 Eichelberger's relationship with MacArthur was strained by several factors: Eichelberger resented the communiqués issued by MacArthur during the battle at Buna. He also was hurt by MacArthur's rejection of the Medal of Honor and his attitude on publicity. Eichelberger was also perplexed by MacArthur's rejection of three requests from Washington to give him command of an army in the European theater.

Eichelberger returned from New Guinea chagrined by three communiqués issued by MacArthur during the Buna-Sanananda campaign. Each misrepresented the conditions at the front and demeaned Eichelberger's contributions. The first described the action at Buna on Christmas Day as "limited to routine safety precautions." This was a blatant lie and Eichelberger could not fathom MacArthur's motive for issuing it. In reality, the fighting at Buna that day was bitter, and Eichelberger suffered heavy casualties. He still had another week of hard fighting before he captured Buna, and he could not afford to call a halt in the fighting.[4]

The second questionable communiqué was issued by MacArthur upon his return to Australia, when he announced that the Papuan campaign was complete except for some "mopping up on Sanananda." Again, this message was not true and was a great disservice to the soldiers required to take the Japanese positions. The Australians had been unable to capture Sanananda for over a month when this statement was issued, and their commander told Eichelberger that it would take at least three more months to capture it. Eichelberger, however, was able to end that campaign in just two weeks. MacArthur, once again, was caught flatfooted by Eichelberger's speed, which helped to exacerbate their relationship.[5]

The communiqué that most disturbed Eichelberger was issued by MacArthur on 8 January 1943. In it, MacArthur stated that the losses in the Papuan campaign had been very low because of MacArthur's refusal to hurry the attack or to allow the Americans to rush the Japanese positions in an unprepared manner. This communiqué was an outright attempt by MacArthur to mislead the American public about the nature of the fighting at Buna. On 13 December 1942 MacArthur had ordered Eichelberger to attack immediately because "Time is fleeting . . . Time is working desperately against us." On 25 December 1942 MacArthur again reminded Eichelberger of the need to hurry his attacks because of time constraints: "Every additional day you give him to dig in is going to cost you just that many more men to dig him out." Despite MacArthur's lie, the casualties had not been light. Eichelberger calculated that one-half of the infantrymen at Buna had been killed or wounded in the fighting. Yet MacArthur's staff, which was responsible for the high casualties, lacked the moral courage to acknowledge their own errors. Eichelberger was not only hurt and offended by these false communiqués, but was also suspicious of the motives and integrity of MacArthur and his staff.[6]

It is not difficult to rationalize why MacArthur issued these communiqués. He was attempting to cover up his own errors and save his reputation. He sent untrained American soldiers against Japanese veterans and demanded a rapid conclusion to the campaign. A correspondent who knew MacArthur well offers another explanation. In December 1942 MacArthur strongly resented President Franklin D. Roosevelt's "Europe First" concept. This strategy had resulted in the Southwest Pacific area's being relegated to a secondary role. Furthermore, the Joint Chief's of Staff in accord with this strategy had allocated much of the nation's resources to Europe. To protest this strategy, MacArthur believed that "he had to win the war every morning in his communiqués." He had to convince the American public that the war in the Pacific could be won quickly if only President Roosevelt and his advisers would release the necessary assets to him.[7]

Although these communiqués offended Eichelberger and caused him to mistrust MacArthur, the publicity at the conclusion of the campaign further alienated the two men. The anonymity of MacArthur's subordinates is a reflection of MacArthur's refusal to share credit for victories won. During the fighting at Buna, MacArthur's headquarters at Port Moresby released a number of headlines that implied that MacArthur was at the front, personally leading his troops. The Australian press, which knew better, praised Eichelberger as the senior American commander at Buna. However, they were not allowed to print his name for "security" reasons. So they ran a number of stories about the heroics of an "unknown general," which further irked MacArthur and his staff. On 9 January 1943 Eichelberger's name was finally released to the press as that "unknown general." Eichelberger knew that MacArthur had been deeply embarrassed by the news that someone else had been doing the fighting at Buna. This embarrassment eventually led to MacArthur's threat to relieve Eichelberger and send him back to the United States.[8]

MacArthur remained sensitive about the fact that he had allowed his staff to publish erroneous press releases on the Buna campaign. Some time later, the renowned author and historian, Douglas Southall Freeman, while doing research for a book he was going to write entitled *MacArthur and His Generals* (a project he later gave up), asked Eichelberger the date when MacArthur had moved his headquarters to Buna. Eichelberger tried to avoid answering the question but finally admitted that MacArthur never was at Buna.

Eichelberger later said in exasperation of the incident: "Now I ask you why MacA[rthur] didn't just tell the truth [and] say he didn't go to Buna."[9]

MacArthur's unwillingness to share the headlines resulted in virtual anonymity for those around him. Eichelberger actively sought to avoid publicity for his subordinates. He told a close friend in the Bureau of Public Relations that he would rather have someone slip a rattlesnake in his pocket that receive any publicity. It should be noted that MacArthur's bizarre attitude over publicity was observed and commented on in Washington. Eichelberger's old mentor, Major General William D. Connor, wrote him about his lack of publicity. He said, "I read all too little of you in the news of the Southwest Pacific. Your gallant chief . . . does not care to have any competition in the press part of his adventures. We read a lot about Douglas but there seem to be no subordinates that merit mention."[10]

Another point of contention with MacArthur was the credit given to the Marine Corps for victory in the Pacific. Since the Marine press agents were not subject to MacArthur's egotistical blue pencil, the public was convinced that the Marine Corps had won the war in the Pacific. Eichelberger understood how it happened. In a joint United States Army and Marine Corps operation, in late 1943, both services were offered the opportunity to take along reporters. The army commander, Major General Clarence Martin (Eichelberger's able assistant at Buna), knowing MacArthur's attitude on publicity, protested that he could not take care of them. The marine commander, on the other hand, gladly accepted all his assigned reporters and stated that "he was willing to take more."[11]

For many reasons Eichelberger's relationship with MacArthur had become strained. However, Eichelberger was a professional soldier who completely understood the military system. MacArthur was the boss. No matter how unfair it might seem, it was Eichelberger's role as the subordinate to get along with his superior's egomania. Eichelberger's professionalism was to be tested even further in 1943. In the first six months after his return from Buna, MacArthur disapproved the award of the Medal of Honor and thwarted three attempts by General George C. Marshall to reward Eichelberger with the command of an army.

MacArthur's actions shocked and dismayed Eichelberger. He would have coveted either. The Medal of Honor, for example, was awarded to only 289 men in World War II. Harry Truman once stated that he would rather have received the Medal of Honor than to have been president of the United States. General George Patton, Eichelberger's classmate, said, "I'd give my immortal soul for that decoration."[12]

Eichelberger's subordinates had been so impressed by his heroism that they had recommended him for this award. He had taken MacArthur's order to "Take Buna or don't come back alive" literally during the Papuan campaign. General Herring, Eichelberger's immediate superior during the Papuan campaign, had become so alarmed at Eichelberger's constant exposure at the front that he had personally requested that MacArthur order Eichelberger to take care of himself before he was killed. MacArthur replied to Herring, "I want him to die if he doesn't get into Buna." MacArthur had never left Port Moresby—despite press releases to the contrary—to visit the front. He was unaware of Eichelberger's problems or exploits. Eichelberger could never understand why MacArthur would override the eyewitness reports from the battlefield and disapprove the recommendation for award of the Medal of Honor. It was an insult that Eichelberger would never forgive—or forget.[13]

Eichelberger had little time to brood about his failure to receive the Medal of Honor, because MacArthur viciously inflicted another insult. As an ambitious career officer, Eichelberger naturally desired to be promoted from command of a corps to command of an army. As previously stated, MacArthur brought in Lieutenant General Walter Krueger from the United States to command the only American army in the theater—a slap at Eichelberger. Less than a month after winning the first ground victory of the Pacific war, he had been passed over for advancement. MacArthur's ego had once again obscured his judgment.

George C. Marshall, the army chief of staff in Washington, thought Eichelberger's performance at Buna had been exemplary and requested that he return to the United States to take command of a newly formed American army. Eichelberger was understandably excited at this prospect and discussed the opportunity with MacArthur, who initially told him, "I wouldn't stand in your way although I believe you would rather stay here and fight." After several months passed and Eichelberger still hadn't received his transfer, he decided to question MacArthur about it. On 29 September

MacArthur met with Eichelberger and admitted that Marshall had twice offered Eichelberger command of an army (the First Army, which went to Lieutenant General Omar Bradley, and the Ninth Army, which was given to Eichelberger's classmate, Lieutenant General William H. Simpson). MacArthur's rationale for his refusal to release Eichelberger was simply to say, "I couldn't admit that I could spare your services, Bob." This action by MacArthur was blatantly unfair. He was purposely blocking Eichelberger's career. Eichelberger had saved MacArthur's reputation at Buna, and his reward was a training assignment in Australia. Not only was MacArthur preventing Eichelberger's promotion to army command, but he was not even utilizing him in combat.

On 21 December 1943 MacArthur turned down a third request by the War Department to give Eichelberger command of an army. Eisenhower had asked Marshall to send Eichelberger to England to command a new army, but MacArthur stymied that opportunity by telling Washington that he needed Eichelberger in the Southwest Pacific because of his "combat experience." MacArthur never bothered to inform Eichelberger that he had turned down the request, and Eichelberger had to hear it at second hand from a friend.[14]

If the true quality of a man can be measured by his courage in the face of adversity, then in 1943 Eichelberger displayed unparalleled patriotism and selfless service to the nation. Despite the estrangement in his relationship with General MacArthur in 1943 and his seemingly dim prospects for future combat, Eichelberger refused to give up. He may have been envious of the promotions and publicity of his classmates and friends in the European theater (like George Patton), but throughout the year his professionalism was unparalleled. He did not angrily reproach MacArthur or create a situation that would be detrimental to the morale or efficiency of the American forces in the theater. Instead he calmly and realistically appraised his relationship with the "American Caesar." He knew that MacArthur respected and admired his ability as a field commander, but he realized MacArthur had an ego problem. In a letter to a close friend, Eichelberger described MacArthur as a "queer combination of a Sarah Bernhardt dominating the stage and, at the same time, fighting off—as he sees it—a great mass of personal enemies, both foreign and domestic, who have no connection with our natural enemy, the Japanese."[15]

Eichelberger believed that a person should obtain a great deal "of inner satisfaction from a job well done." So he set an example for all his subordinates in the theater to emulate. MacArthur had assigned him the mission of training the Twenty-fourth, Thirty-second, and Forty-first divisions for combat, and he threw himself into this task with the dedication and commitment of a fanatic. Throughout 1943 he was haunted by the specter of Buna. In the harsh fighting there, he had learned to respect the tenacity and fighting ability of the Japanese soldier. He had also seen firsthand the cost in American lives of an inadequate training program. During the fighting at Buna, Eichelberger had described to MacArthur the impact of in-adequate training on the battle:

> The regiments of the 32nd Division needed training in the simple things such as scouting and patrolling. We saw these things the first time we went to Tambourine and reported their battle efficiency as low. In scouting and patrolling, for example, lieutenants have been found to take out patrols, stay for a while in the grass, and come back with a full report of a certain area that they have never been near.[16]

Eichelberger believed that the soldiers in both divisions (Thirty-second and Forty-first) had not been prepared mentally for their deployment into combat at Buna. He was convinced that "nothing was further in their minds than the idea that sometime they would leave Australia on an offensive mission." Eichelberger's assessments, before and during the battle, of the shortcomings of the American soldiers led him to institute training programs to ensure that those under his command never again entered battle unprepared for the rigors of combat.

Eichelberger's experience at Buna showed him that American soldiers needed small-unit combat training that emphasized scouting, patrolling, fire control, and security measures. He was sure that this training, combined with an effective chain of command, would produce a highly effective combat unit. In typical Eichelberger fashion, he went down to the units and explained to his soldiers the purpose and rationale behind his training program. In a personal talk to the Twenty-fourth Division, he extolled the importance of small-unit training and said, "Time and again the simple everyday principles that you have learned in training was the difference between success and failure in battle [at Buna]." Eichelberger reinforced this point by using specific incidents from Buna to explain his training program:

> On one occasion I told the commander of a force on the left flank to go into a certain place and find out what was there. He said he couldn't get the men to go into that place. I asked him if he realized that what I was asking him to do was nothing more than simple scouting and patrolling. He said "oh!" as though he was greatly surprised and went out and got the information.

Eichelberger then told the soldiers:

> Another simple thing in all your training is fire control. Yet, how well I remember when a patrol of about 70 men were sent out to guard one flank . . . A small group of Japanese began firing at this force, . . . whereupon these men opened up with all their weapons and quickly fired up all the ammunition they had without seeing anything to shoot at. Having fired all the ammunition they promptly retreated in some disorder.

Eichelberger also stressed the importance of security:

> Security seems to be a simple thing. Yet it is of the utmost importance in fighting an enemy as cunning and aggressive as the Japanese. There were cases when guards would fail to fire on small groups of Japanese because they were afraid the Japanese would return their fire.

Eichelberger concluded his remarks to the Twenty-fourth Division in this way:

> The fact that your training will bear fruit in battle could be illustrated by many true stories. For example, let me tell you about "G" Company, 127th Infantry . . . This company was the spearhead of the drive to the sea. It demonstrated such teamwork, such skill that nothing could stop them. I found out that this company had been the outstanding company in small unit combat training before the unit had left Australia. Small unit training was here paying dividends.[17]

Eichelberger was determined that the mistakes made at Buna would not be repeated. To ensure that his training program was understood and properly executed, he personally supervised its implementation to impress upon his subordinate commanders the importance he placed on small-unit training. In a letter to his new superior, General Krueger (the Sixth Army commander), in July 1943, Eichelberger described the dramatic improvements in combat efficiency of the Thirty-second Division, which had taken place in just six months as a result of his training program:

> Only one company of twenty-one tested was found unsatisfactory. There seems to be fine morale and a lot of enthusiasm . . . I thought the work of certain companies in night attack with accompanying night reconnaissance work was unusually good. The work of other companies in defense accompanied with infiltration and a night withdrawal was not as good.[18]

Eichelberger hammered home to each of his division commanders the value of small-unit training. Prior to combat, each of his divisions devoted half their training time to small-unit tactical problems.[19]

Eichelberger also stressed the importance of developing initiative within the chain of command. His training philosophy reflected the maxim that "The amount of initiative officers (and men) display in war will probably be in direct proportion to the effort made to inculcate it in peacetime training."[20] Eichelberger's attitudes on the importance of initiative and a strong chain of command were clearly influenced by his experiences at Buna. In the midst of the fighting there, he had admonished Major General Horace Fuller, saying, "You will find that you must follow the chain of command. Develop sergeants and corporals that will really take charge of their men." In another letter he advised Fuller that "One of the greatest difficulties we find up here is a shortage of junior officers and noncommissioned officers with guts and ability to lead small units." Eichelberger realized that in the chaos of combat, especially in the jungle, it was necessary to decentralize authority to the lowest levels of leadership. This meant that, many times, the success of a battle depended on the courage and initiative of junior officers and noncommissioned officers. They would be the ones who would discover and exploit the vulnerabilities of the enemy. However, this would happen in battle only if this initiative was inculcated during training.[21]

An excellent example of Eichelberger's philosophy is contained in a letter written by his deputy chief of staff, Colonel Rex Chandler. At forty-two, Chandler was a young, handsome, and extremely brilliant staff officer who worked closely with Eichelberger. As a confidant, Chandler completely understood Eichelberger's rationale for stressing the chain of command and he passed it on to his brother, Second Lieutenant Oscar W. Chandler:

> The next item is what Eichelberger calls the chain of command and the responsibility of every officer and noncommissioned officer in the chain. Hold the sergeant responsible for his section and all its equipment, to include the gun truck. Hold the lieutenant responsible for his platoon, and so on. When you see something wrong don't correct the individual soldier. Give the sergeant hell for failing to see trouble before you did and make him correct it.[22]

Eichelberger's emphasis on a strong chain of command was not a new idea. Rather, it was a commonsense response to a serious deficiency noted at Buna, where the chain of command's inefficiency in inspecting, supervising, and enforcing discipline had been one of the most glaring causes of the division's initial failure. This experience led Eichelberger to the conclusion that nothing of importance should ever be left to the discretion of the individual soldier. He believed that specific instructions should be issued and enforced on such diverse subjects as the "taking of quinine, the care of insect bites, the maintenance of weapons, shaving and bathing and avoidance of sleeping on the ground." Eichelberger had observed at Buna that those units in which leaders had enforced standards of discipline, cleanliness, and maintenance of equipment were the units with the highest morale, efficiency, and fighting spirit.[23]

Eichelberger also insisted upon conditioning his troops for the environmental and situational factors they would encounter in battle. He realized that all future operations would have to be conducted in the jungle, and that the American soldier was not naturally prepared for this environment. Anticipating numerous streams, swamps, and rivers, Eichelberger insisted that the soldiers learn how to swim and that all units conduct extensive training in stream-crossing operations. Since the jungle would be an extremely demanding environment physically, Eichelberger instituted a physical-hardening program, which included forced marches, hand-to-hand combat, bayonet training, and obstacle courses. He knew that the physically conditioned soldiers could deal with the fatigue that breeds fear and defeatism.[24]

Eichelberger's training program also prepared the soldier to fight in the jungle at night. The Japanese spent a great deal of time on night training. This had been a major weakness of the Thirty-second Division at Buna. As previously noted, that division had conducted only one night-training exercise in the twenty months before deploying to combat. Therefore Eichelberger had his troops conduct extensive small-unit night training in such operations as night raids, night attacks, night defenses, night withdrawals, and night infiltrations. To add realism to these operations and to prepare his soldiers for the noise and confusion of the battlefield, he had the artillery fire live ammunition overhead. This tough and realistic training gave Eichelberger's soldiers confidence in their own abilities. The more demanding and exhausting the conditions, the better prepared they would be for the stress of combat. In this difficult training environment, he built a cohesive and proficient battle unit.

In preparing his soldiers for every type of situation, Eichelberger also conducted extensive day and night training in amphibious operations. Realizing that all future operations would commence with an amphibious landing, he devoted much training to this type of warfare under as realistic conditions as possible.[25]

Throughout all of 1943 Eichelberger remained in Australia, training the three divisions of I Corps. He watched over every aspect of the planning and execution of the training program with an almost religious fanaticism. He constantly visited the training sites and would teach, counsel, coach, and critique while passing on his experiences from Buna. If he was disappointed by MacArthur's treatment, he never showed it. His devotion to building I Corps into a formidable fighting machine capable of successfully accomplishing any future assignment was noticed by his superiors. Both MacArthur and Krueger, during training inspections, were greatly impressed by the high standards of efficiency and morale in the I Corps. In fact, Krueger was so impressed by the improvement in the Thirty-second Division that in October 1943 he placed this unit under the direct control of his own staff. He then used elements of this division, with great success, to conduct the invasion of Saidor on 2 January 1944.

Eichelberger, although he did not lead this unit in battle, took a great deal of pride in their accomplishments because of his personal training program.[26]

While the Twenty-fourth and Forty-first divisions had received the maximum benefit from Eichelberger's training, they were not able to prove their effectiveness until their deployment to combat in April 1944.

MacArthur did not conduct any corps-sized operations in 1943, but he did conduct smaller operations that neutralized Rabaul, the Japanese stronghold, which contained 145,000 Japanese soldiers. To accomplish this mission, MacArthur decided against a frontal assault, as he had conducted at Buna, and opted for a series of envelopments. He would apply his strength against the Japanese weaknesses. He would avoid the front, where they could best concentrate their fires, and attack their flank. He sought to cut the Japanese line of communication—the air, sea, and land routes over which reinforcements and supplies flow—to prevent their reinforcement or escape.[27]

MacArthur first employed his strategy of side-stepping heavily fortified Japanese positions by outflanking and severing their logistical lifelines in September 1943. On 11 September Salamaua was seized, and on 16 September Lae was captured. MacArthur was able to neutralize the powerful Japanese base at Rabaul, in 1943, without conducting a costly frontal assault. He accomplished this by seizing important airfields at Finschafen in October, on Bougainville in November, and at Cape Gloucester in December 1943. The landing at Saidor on 2 January 1944 and the successful invasion of the Admiralty Islands on 29 February 1944 completed the isolation of the Japanese garrison at Rabaul.[28]

The Japanese stronghold at Rabaul had been isolated at a minimum cost in American lives. The airplanes that flew from newly built airfields cut the air and sea routes in and out of Rabaul. A powerful army was stuck at Rabaul and was unable to participate in any future operations. In reality, the only thing this army did for the rest of the war was to try and fight off starvation.

The neutralization of the Japanese garrison put MacArthur in an excellent position to continue his drive up the northern coast of New Guinea. But MacArthur's pace had been very slow. The Japanese had established a number of large, powerful bases along the northern coast of New Guinea, and each of these had to be neutralized.

Despite the successful operations of 1943, the Allies had advanced only 240 miles up the coast of New Guinea. MacArthur still had 2,240 miles to go before he reached Manila. At his present pace, the war in the Pacific would last another ten years. MacArthur realized that if he did not step up his pace, Washington would send the bulk of the nation's resources to Europe and aid him only after the defeat of Germany.

For all his personal flaws, MacArthur's ability as a strategist has never been questioned. His plan for increasing the tempo of the campaign was brilliant. Using a tactic that would stand him well at Inchon, Korea, some six years later, MacArthur proposed an amphibious landing that leapfrogged the Japanese. His plan was strongly endorsed by General George C. Marshall, the chief of staff, and on 12 March 1944 the Joint Chiefs of Staff approved MacArthur's plan to land troops at Hollandia, 600 miles up the coast of New Guinea. In one maneuver he would bypass the heavily fortified Japanese garrisons at Hansa Bay, Wewak, and Madang, leaving them isolated and vulnerable.[29] In supporting MacArthur's plan, General Marshall wisely observed that "a democracy cannot fight a seven years war." The Hollandia operation was to be triple the pace of all the operations conducted the previous year. The Joint Chiefs of Staff also granted MacArthur permission to continue his advance up the coast of New Guinea as soon as he had occupied and developed a base at Hollandia. They further advised him to be prepared to invade the Philippines as soon as New Guinea was secured.[30]

MacArthur's selection of Hollandia as his next target was a stroke of pure genius. The Hollandia landing site was broken by two deep indentations at Humboldt and Tanahmerah bays, which were twenty-five miles apart. The Cyclops Mountains, a range that reached a height of 7,000 feet, was between the two bays. The crucial area in this operation was the valley just south of the Cyclops Mountains, between the two bays, where the Japanese had built three airstrips. Once taken, American aircraft could use these airfields to neutralize other Japanese air bases in western New Guinea. In addition, MacArthur's future advances in New Guinea and those of Admiral Chester Nimitz in the western Carolines could be supported from these airfields.[31]

Hollandia had a huge natural harbor capable of supporting the largest combat and support ships in the United States Navy. This harbor was the only sheltered anchorage in western New Guinea before Geelvink Bay. Once taken, Hollandia could be built into a huge logistical base to support future offensives along the northern coast of New Guinea and for the proposed invasion of the Philippines.[32]

Aside from geographical considerations, there were important strategic reasons for selecting Hollandia as a landing site. MacArthur could count on the element of surprise in this operation. He would be striking the Japanese at a place where they definitely would not expect him. The Japanese had stationed their Thirty-sixth Division in the Wakde-Sarmi region and the Fifty-first Division at Wewak. The 300 miles of coast that lay between these two strongholds were largely undefended. Although the Japanese had commenced to build Hollandia into a major logistical base and had built three airfields on the Lake Sentani plain, only the Sixth Air Division and some support troops had been stationed at Hollandia. The Japanese commander in the theater had assumed, since MacArthur had advanced only as far as Saidor by mid-April 1944, that the next landing would be another short jump to Hansa Bay or Wewak. He had seriously underestimated MacArthur, and he would pay dearly for his error.[33]

MacArthur fully realized that the amphibious landing at Hollandia was a daring and ambitious undertaking. He needed a powerful enough force to seize his objective before the Japanese could react. He decided to land an entire corps at Hollandia, because failure there would seriously retard his timetable. MacArthur had sold Washington the merits of this operation and he could not afford to fail. To ensure success, MacArthur and Krueger selected the theater's most able field commander to lead the operation—Robert Eichelberger.

After fourteen months of training troops in Australia, Eichelberger was again assigned the theater's most important and difficult operation. This time he would go into battle with troops he trained himself, the Twenty-fourth and Forty-first divisions. Also, he would draw up his own plan of attack, unlike at Buna where he had inherited someone else's. This time Eichelberger was determined to avoid a drawn-out campaign, like Buna, and quickly to destroy the Japanese.

MacArthur demanded a lot from Eichelberger at Hollandia. His mission was more complex than it might appear at first glance. Eichelberger was expected to establish a beachhead, defeat a sizable Japanese force, and advance inland twenty miles to seize the three airfields. This was only the tip of the iceberg. Eichelberger was then expected to build Hollandia into a major logistical base capable of supporting MacArthur's next two operations in the advance to the Philippines—the Toem-Sarmi landing on 15 May 1944, and the 27 May 1944 invasion of Biak. These two operations were MacArthur's last on the northern coast of New Guinea. If successful, MacArthur could commence his invasion of the Philippines.[34]

Eichelberger's Hollandia task force, code-named "Reckless Task Force," consisted of the Twenty-fourth and Forty-first divisions (less the 163rd Regimental Combat Team) plus supplementary support units. Each division had been vigorously trained by Eichelberger to ensure that the problems encountered at Buna were not repeated. The total command strength for this operation was 37,527 combat troops and 18,184 service troops. On 15 March 1944 Eichelberger briefed his subordinates. At this meeting Major General Frederick Irving and the Twenty-fourth Division were assigned responsibility for the Tanahmerah Bay landing. Major General Horace Fuller and the Forty-first Division were assigned the Humboldt Bay landing. D–Day was set for 22 April 1944. Once ashore, both division were to push inland as rapidly as possible to seize the airstrips.[35]

Eichelberger's attack on 22 April 1944 was meticulously planned. At Tanahmerah Bay, the Twenty-fourth Division was to land on two beaches. The main force was to land at Red Beach 2. A single battalion was to land at Red Beach 1 in Depapre Bay and secure a precipitous narrow trail, the only road between Tanahmerah Bay and the three airfields. The United States Navy had wanted to cancel the landing on Red Beach 1 because they thought it was unnecessary; however, Eichelberger kept it in at General Irving's request. The landing at Tanahmerah Bay was one pincer and the landing at Humboldt Bay the other. Eichelberger envisioned both pincers rapidly slicing through the Japanese and linking up on the airfields.[36]

The key to success in this operation would be speed. Eichelberger did not want to get bogged down in a siege as had occurred at Buna. That type of battle always results in attrition and high casualties. Instead, Eichelberger wanted his troops to take full advantage of surprise and to move so fast that the enemy would be kept off balance and unable to present a coherent defense. The Japanese, he believed, should not be allowed to recover from their shock. He hoped to break through their defenses and seize the airfields before they could react.[37]

Eichelberger was very fortunate to have two excellent division commanders for the Hollandia operation. Major General Frederick Irving was a protégé of Eichelberger. He had served as commandant of cadets when Eichelberger had been the superintendent at West Point. Although forty-nine, he did not appear to have put on a single pound of fat since his days as the brigade boxing champion at West Point. Irving was quiet, efficient, and unassuming, but Eichelberger knew he had the heart of a warrior. As a young officer in World War I, Irving had led his company through a withering storm of artillery and machine-gun fire to seize an objective. He had been seriously wounded and had earned the Silver Star. Eichelberger knew that in combat Irving would be unstoppable.

Eichelberger's other division commander was the ever reliable Horace Fuller. Fuller was Eichelberger's West Point classmate and was intensely loyal. He did not resent working for a friend. Fuller was short and thin, and a cigarette was constantly dangling from his lips. Eichelberger had been impressed by the performance of the Forty-first Division at Sanananda, and knew that Fuller would perform well. Both these commanders had been thoroughly indoctrinated with the lessons Eichelberger had learned at Buna. Both were fighters who would lead by example.[38]

Eichelberger never took anything for granted. In the three weeks before D–Day at Hollandia, he pushed his troops harder than ever. He continued his demanding training program and emphasized physical hardening, more small-unit tactics, and amphibious training. Eichelberger was meticulous in ensuring that his troops would be ready for combat. Because the army had not had much training with naval gunfire, he instituted a program of integrating naval shore-fire control parties with artillery personnel. Up to the time his troops boarded the assault ships, Eichelberger gave them every training advantage to avoid repeating the mistakes of Buna.[39]

Eichelberger's attention to detail, and close supervision in the planning of this operation, paid off in the smooth adjustment to unexpected developments during the battle. He was also a shrewd judge of human nature. Knowing that soldiers perform best when they have an opportunity to comment on a plan, he incorporated the ideas of both landing-force commanders into his final plan. So closely did he supervise the preparations for this operation that one regimental journal laconically noted that "meetings were as frequent as meals." Before his troops boarded their ships to sail for Hollandia,

Eichelberger personally conducted and critiqued a dress rehearsal of the amphibious landing.[40]

Shortly after dawn on 22 April 1944 the United States Navy simultaneously landed two regiments of the Twenty-fourth Division at Tanahmerah Bay and two regiments of the Forty-first Division at Humboldt Bay. The Hollandia operation had begun. The loading and unloading of the landing craft and the seizure of the beachheads were conducted flawlessly. Eichelberger, with a great deal of satisfaction, later described the landings as follows: "Our long training in amphibious assault was rewarded. The landings were classical in their precision. Down to the most minute detail of planning, everything went off as scheduled."[41]

At Humboldt Bay the two regiments of the Forty-first Division (162nd and 186th Regimental Combat Teams) landed at four separate beaches. General Fuller, who agreed with Eichelberger's philosophy that a leader must set a personal example for his men, came ashore at 1005 hours and rapidly pushed his forces inland. The Japanese forces at Humboldt Bay were so completely surprised that they fled from the beach area. The lead patrols of the Forty-first Division moved so rapidly that at the Japanese headquarters they found teapots that were still boiling and breakfast bowls of rice only half eaten.[42]

The situation at Tanahmerah Bay was not so good. The Twenty-fourth Division landed its troops at Red Beach 1 and 2, as planned. Tactical surprise was complete in this area, too. However, at Red Beach 2, which was to have been the main landing site, a serious Intelligence error had occurred and a waist-deep swamp prevented traffic inland. It turned out that the beach was only thirty yards deep and the swamp was impenetrable. That day, as successive waves of men and equipment came in, things began piling up on the beach. Because the supplies could not be moved inland, the situation there soon became a nightmare.[43]

The situation was far different on Red Beach 1. Lieutenant Colonel Thomas E. Clifford and the First Battalion, Twenty-first Infantry quickly established a beachhead. Thomas E. (Jock) Clifford was an extraordinary leader. He had been an All-American football player at West Point and was a dynamic personality. He ran his battalion like a team. They called themselves "Clifford's Cowboys." At age thirty-two Clifford was in excellent physical condition and personally set a high example for his men. He was an excellent motivator and very skillful in dealing with people. In the training of his battalion he acted as teacher, coach, and counselor. He was an aggressive and tenacious leader and instilled these attitudes in his men. His was one of the best-trained battalions in the army, and his men idolized him.[44]

Eichelberger hoped that his training program would develop subordinates with audacity and initiative, capable of acting independently to accomplish the goals of higher headquarters. Eichelberger was not disappointed by Jock Clifford. Clifford did not sit on the beach; rather, he displayed great initiative and quickly moved his unit, without waiting for reinforcements, up a steep cliff to a trail that led toward the airfields that were the division's objectives. The long hours of grueling physical training paid handsome dividends as the soldiers were able to negotiate the sixty-degree slope and push rapidly inland. Despite the harsh jungle terrain and the constant fear of enemy contact, the physically fit unit, which had trained in the jungle, covered six miles that day. That night the battalion halted and prepared a defensive position. So highly trained was the unit in night operations, that the Japanese night attack on their positions failed to dent the perimeter. In fact, after this failed night attack, the Japanese made no further attempt to cut the trail behind the First Battalion, Twenty-first Infantry. This encounter, unlike that at Buna, found the Americans more skilled at jungle warfare and night operations than the Japanese.[45]

A War Department observer of this phase of the operation, Colonel Edwin Carns, reported to General George C. Marshall that the "planning and execution were outstanding in the Hollandia operation." Carns was also impressed by the initiative displayed by members of the chain of command when they encountered unexpected difficulties. General Irving's leadership style was similar to that of Eichelberger; he went to the location of the problem in order to make the best possible decision. After viewing the confusion on Red Beach 2, caused by the swamps, he immediately began shifting the remainder of the Twenty-first Regiment to Red Beach 1. This regiment was commanded by Colonel Charles B. Lyman. At fifty-six, Lyman was one of the oldest colonels commanding an infantry regiment in the army. He was an affable, easygoing socialite known for his love of horses. He came from a distinguished family and his father was the first lieutenant governor of Hawaii. Lyman was a thoroughly professional infantry officer. He had graduated from

## Buna Avenged and Another Fire

West Point in 1913 and from the Command and General Staff School and the Army War College. He served in a variety of infantry assignments for thirty-one years. So thoroughly trained were his troops, and so detailed was the planning of the landing operation, that two-and-a-half hours later, at 1300, Colonel Lyman and the remainder of his regiment were on Red Beach 1, ready to exploit the success of Jock Clifford's First Battalion.[46]

Eichelberger personally visited both landing sites on 22 April. After viewing the logistical problems on Red Beach 2, he modified his tactical plan and made Humboldt Bay the principal task-force landing site, and the emphasis of the attack shifted to the inland drive of the Forty-first Division. In support of this decision, on D + 1, Eichelberger shifted his reserve (Thirty-fourth Regimental Combat Team) and all D + 2 convoys to Humboldt Bay. At the same time, however, Eichelberger continued to exploit the success of the now consolidated Twenty-first Regiment's drive inland from Tanahmerah Bay.[47]

Unlike his action at Buna, MacArthur personally came ashore at Hollandia at 1100 hours on 22 April 1944. He inspected the Forty-first Division beachhead at Humboldt Bay and talked with General Fuller. He was greatly impressed by the success and morale of that unit. At 1500 hours MacArthur landed at Tanahmerah Bay and conferred briefly with General Irving at Red Beach 2. Although there was a great deal of confusion on the beach, MacArthur apparently did not realize the problems that had been created by the swamp or the necessity of shifting the emphasis of the attack.[48]

Flushed with victory, MacArthur called a special staff meeting late on the afternoon of 22 April aboard his cruiser, the U. S. S. *Nashville*. MacArthur invited Rear Admiral Daniel Barbey, Lieutenant General Walter Krueger, Brigadier General George Decker (chief of staff, Sixth Army), Colonel Clyde Eddleman (operations officer, Sixth Army), Brigadier General Clovis Byers (chief of staff, I Corps), and Lieutenant General Eichelberger. MacArthur was so impressed by what he had observed at the beachheads that he concluded that the Hollandia operation was successfully completed. He ordered Eichelberger to move 100 miles further up the coast of New Guinea to seize Toem-Sarmi within seventy-two hours. This operation was scheduled to take place on 15 May and to be supported by air cover from the Hollandia airfields. When neither Admiral Barbey nor General Krueger attempted to dissuade MacArthur, Eichelberger felt compelled to protest. He pointed out that the Japanese strength had not yet been tested and that the airfields, his primary objective, had not yet been captured. Eichelberger further argued that the ships were all loaded to support subsequent landings at Hollandia, and were not properly loaded to support the Toem-Sarmi landing. Because of Hollandia, it would take longer than seventy-two hours to reload and restock these ships. As a result of Eichelberger's vehement opposition, MacArthur decided to conduct the Toem-Sarmi operation as originally planned.[49]

Admiral Barbey, who was present at this conference, later reproached Eichelberger for his caution. Barbey wrote that "Eichelberger still had bloody memoirs of the Japanese capabilities in the Buna campaign . . . as he was to learn later, however, their capabilities had greatly deteriorated since those hard-fought days." Although Admiral Barbey's assessment of the enemy's capabilities was correct at Hollandia (there was minimal opposition), as will be seen at Biak, Eichelberger's respect for the Japanese proved well founded.[50]

Back on shore at Hollandia, the flawless execution of the landing phase had completely surprised the Japanese at both Humboldt and Tanahmerah bays. The initiative displayed by Colonel Clifford and the flexibility of the Twenty-fourth Division's staff allowed the momentum of the Tanahmerah pincer to be sustained. On both flanks the discipline and training of the individual soldier paid handsome dividends. The Japanese were never able to gain the initiative or to reconstruct a defense. Eichelberger later wrote that "for the soldiers making the pincer movement on the dromes [airfields], there was nothing for it except slog, slog, slog. Fuller's troops [Forty-first Division] had twenty-one miles to go; Irving's troops [Twenty-fourth Division] had only fourteen miles to go, but their going was harder. They had fourteen streams to cross." Eichelberger's soldiers were prepared for this challenge, thanks to his physical-training program and long hours of stream-crossing rehearsal. Neither the terrain nor the enemy slowed the advance. The Americans relentlessly and aggressively pushed to their objectives. By 1645 hours on 27 April, the tactical phase of the operation ended when patrols of the Forty-first Division linked up with those from the Twenty-fourth Division on the northeast corner of the third and final airfield.[51]

The demanding training program devised by Eichelberger after Buna was a resounding success at Hollandia. The landings were flawless. The initiative displayed by subordinate commanders and the physical toughness of the troops enabled the operation to continue despite the obstacles on one landing beach. The violent execution at the beachhead ruptured the Japanese defenses. The vigorous advance by the American infantry prevented the Japanese from reconstituting their defenses. The realistic training had prepared every soldier in both divisions for the rigors of combat. Eichelberger had every right to be proud of his training program and of his soldiers. He had captured Hollandia in only five days. He had avenged Buna; it was the Japanese who knew fear.

It is important to recognize the difference in quality of the Japanese forces at Buna and Hollandia. On the morning of 22 April 1944, there were 11,000 Japanese at Hollandia. MacArthur's Intelligence officer, General Willoughby, believed that one Japanese marine regiment and two veteran infantry regiments were stationed at Hollandia. Eichelberger's decision to protest the move to Toem-Sarmi on the afternoon of 22 April was based on this information. However, Willoughby's information, as usual, was very inaccurate. There were only poorly trained service troops at Hollandia. These Japanese troops were unable to form any kind of defense against the highly trained soldiers of I Corps. At a cost of 124 American lives, Eichelberger's soldiers killed 3,000 Japanese and captured 611. The remaining 7,000 Japanese fled into the jungle. Their commander, General Masazumi Inada, attempted a march of 125 miles through the jungle to link up with the Japanese garrison at Wakde. On 30 April these troops started their march, without food or maps. More than 6,000 Japanese soldiers died in the attempt.[52]

On 28 April, with the three airfields captured, Eichelberger's job had just begun. His greatest enemy was now time. His job was one of construction. Eichelberger was responsible for ensuring that the engineers prepare the three airfields to launch army fighter planes and bombers in support of the Wakde invasion (15 May) and the Biak operation (27 May). He had to construct a road from Humboldt Bay to all three airfields and 135 miles of pipeline to pump gasoline from the bay to the airfields. Docks had to be constructed in Humboldt Bay to unload the supply ships, and Hollandia had to be built into a logistical base capable of supporting 140,000 support troops.[53]

Eichelberger possessed the experience, breadth of knowledge, and imagination to accomplish this difficult task. He set an impressive example for his subordinates. He got up very early each morning and made a point of visiting construction activities in the harbors and at the airfields. He did this to show the hard-working construction troops that he knew what they were accomplishing and that he cared about them. His close supervision also enabled him to smooth over any coordination problems and to avoid misconceptions about responsibility between units. Every evening, sometimes long after midnight, he held meetings with the engineers to set priorities and allocate resources. He had to coordinate between units, evaluate performance, counsel those units or commanders with problems, and generally act as a coach for the entire logistical build-up. MacArthur was able to conduct the Wakde (15 May), Biak (27 May), and Noemfoor (2 July) operations from the impressive logistical base Eichelberger built at Hollandia.[54]

Despite all the pressure Eichelberger was under to complete the logistical requirements at Hollandia, he never forgot the individual needs of his soldiers. He knew how to take care of his men. He decorated both Fuller and Irving with the Silver Star for gallantry in action. He realized that medals were very important to a soldier psychologically and had a great deal of motivational power. They were tangible evidence of a soldier's courage and achievement. The awards given to Fuller and Irving were not only recognition for a job well done, but a gentle reminder that they should recognize the contributions of the men in their respective commands.[55]

The Hollandia operation was officially concluded on 6 June 1944. During this entire campaign, Eichelberger did not once come into conflict with MacArthur over publicity or method of execution. However, his conduct of this operation did significantly enhance his reputation for efficiency and leadership throughout the American army. The chief of staff of the army, George C. Marshall, called the Hollandia operation a model of strategic and tactical maneuver.[56]

Eichelberger did not have much of an opportunity to relax after the Hollandia operation. Another fire was raging in the Southwest Pacific and it again threatened to engulf MacArthur's reputation. An American invasion force had been stopped cold on Biak Island, and MacArthur needed a new field commander to go in and salvage the tactical situation. MacArthur wanted this problem handled quickly, so he sent in his best—Robert L. Eichelberger.

Biak was a small coral island 300 miles west of Hollandia, upon which the Japanese had built three airfields. MacArthur hoped to

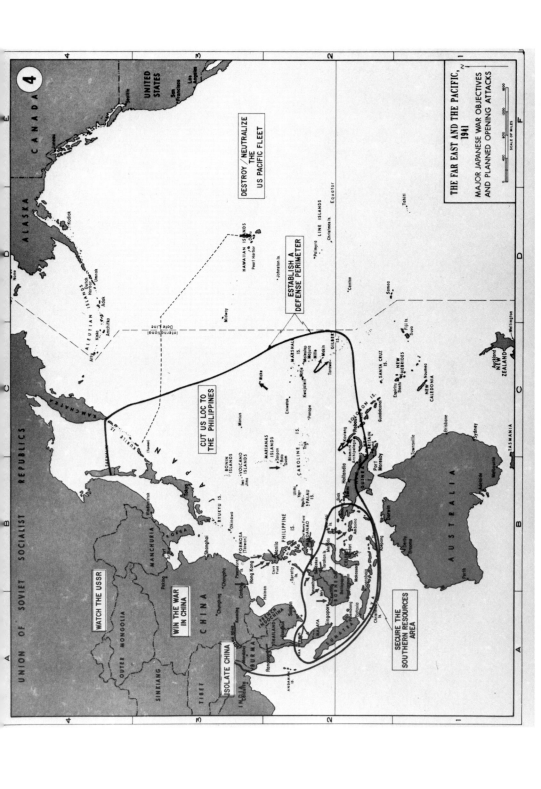

4

THE FAR EAST AND THE PACIFIC, 1941

MAJOR JAPANESE WAR OBJECTIVES AND PLANNED OPENING ATTACKS

SCALE OF MILES

DESTROY / NEUTRALIZE THE US PACIFIC FLEET

ESTABLISH A DEFENSE PERIMETER

CUT US LOC TO THE PHILIPPINES

WATCH THE USSR

WIN THE WAR IN CHINA

ISOLATE CHINA

SECURE THE SOUTHERN RESOURCES AREA

UNITED STATES

CANADA

ALASKA

UNION OF SOVIET SOCIALIST REPUBLICS

OUTER MONGOLIA

SINKIANG

TIBET

MANCHURIA

CHINA

KOREA

BURMA

THAILAND

FRENCH INDOCHINA

MALAYA

SUMATRA

BORNEO

AUSTRALIA

NEW ZEALAND

TASMANIA

PHILIPPINE IS.

FORMOSA (Taiwan)

RYUKYU IS.

Okinawa

ALEUTIAN ISLANDS

International Date Line

HAWAIIAN ISLANDS

Pearl Harbor

Midway

Johnston Is.

Wake

MARIANAS ISLANDS

Saipan

Guam

CAROLINE IS.

PALAU IS.

VOLCANO ISLANDS

Iwo Jima

BONIN ISLANDS

MARSHALL IS.

Kwajalein

Eniwetok

GILBERT IS.

Makin

Tarawa

Ponape

Truk

Wotje

Majuro

Mili

SOLOMON IS.

Rabaul

NEW BRITAIN

Bismarck Archipelago

NEW GUINEA

Port Moresby

Buna

Hollandia

SANTA CRUZ IS.

NEW HEBRIDES

Guadalcanal

Espiritu Santo

NEW CALEDONIA

Noumea

Fiji Is.

Suva

Samoa

Canton

LINE ISLANDS

Palmyra

Christmas Is.

Equator

Tahiti

Wellington

Auckland

Sydney

Melbourne

Adelaide

Perth

Brisbane

Townsville

Darwin

Seattle

San Francisco

Los Angeles

KAMCHATKA

Vladivostok

Shanghai

Hong Kong

Hainan

Manila

Singapore

Bangkok

Rangoon

Chungking

Nome

Kodiak

Nanking

Peiping

KURILE IS.

Sakhalin

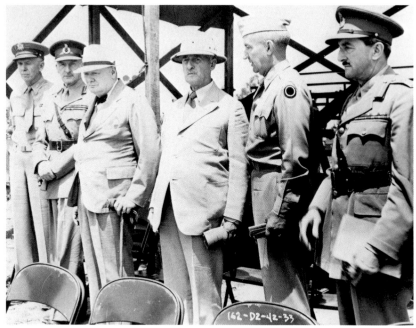

Reviewing party at the demonstration for Winston Churchill, 24 June 1942. *Left to right:* General George C. Marshall, Chief of Staff, U.S. Army; Field Marshal Sir John Dill; Prime Minister Winston Churchill, U.S. Secretary of War Henry L. Stimson; Major General Robert Eichelberger, Commanding General, I Corps; General Sir Alan Brooke, Britain's Chief of Staff (U.S. Army Photo).

Eichelberger conducts a working lunch with his staff (U.S. Army Photo).

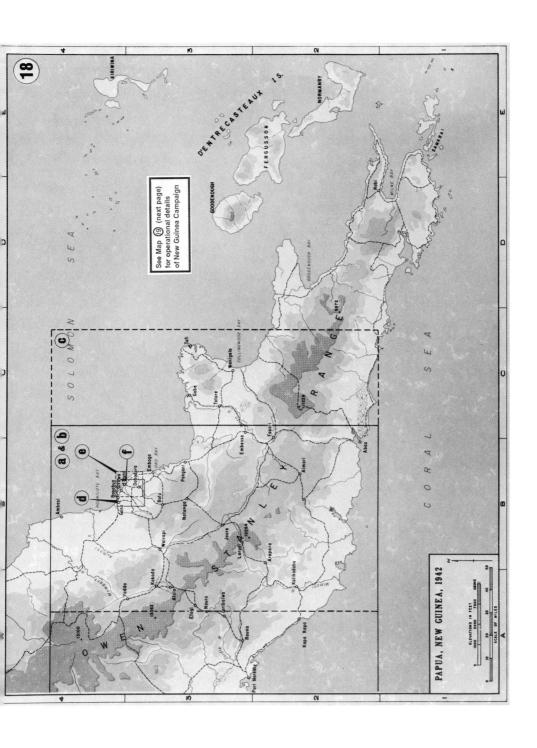

18

KIRIWINA

SOLOMON SEA

D'ENTRECASTEAUX IS.

See Map ⑲ (next page)
for operational details
of New Guinea Campaign

GOODENOUGH

FERGUSSON

NORMANBY

SAMARAI

MILNE BAY

GOODENOUGH BAY

COLLINGWOOD BAY

ⓒ

Tufi

Gobe

Totore

Wanigela

11226

RANGE

Faseri

Abao

CORAL SEA

ⓐ & ⓑ

ⓔ

ⓕ

ⓓ

Ambasi

Gona

Sanananda
Buna
Dobodura

Embogo
Buda

HOLNICOTE BAY

DYKE ACKLAND BAY

Soputa

Popondetta

Emboge

Pongani

Aimuri

Natunga

Embessi

STANLEY

Wairopi

Joure

Kokoda

Abiol

Eroro

Nauro

Uberi

Menari

Isurava

Laruni

Alora

Kagi

Myola

Efogi

13363

Kokoda

OWEN

13100

Kaipit

Kopa Kopa

Rouna

Koiiitodobu

Port Moresby

Kuni

Kapa Kapa

PAPUA, NEW GUINEA, 1942

ELEVATIONS IN FEET
1000  2000  7000  ABOVE

SCALE OF MILES
0   10   20   30   40   50

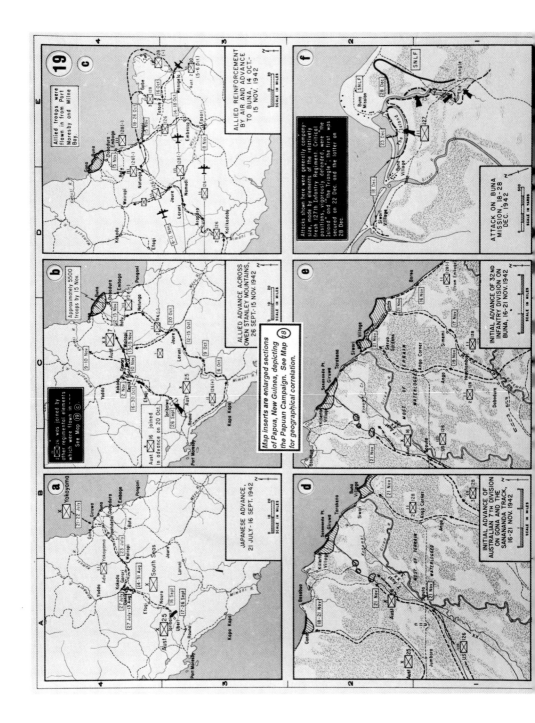

**19**

**c** Allied troops were flown in from Port Moresby and Milne Bay.

ALLIED REINFORCEMENT BY AIR AND ADVANCE TO BUNA, 14 OCT.-15 NOV. 1942

SCALE IN MILES

**f** Attacks shown here were generally company-sized, made by elements of the relatively fresh 127th Infantry Regiment. Critical positions, vigorously defended, were "the Island" and "the Triangle"; the first was secured on 22 Dec. and the latter on 28 Dec.

ATTACK ON BUNA MISSION, 18-28 DEC. 1942

SCALE IN YARDS

**b**
Approximately 5500 troops by 15 Nov.

ALLIED ADVANCE ACROSS OWEN STANLEY MOUNTAINS, 26 SEPT.-15 NOV. 1942

SCALE IN MILES

25 was joined by other regimental elements which were flown in ---
See Map 19 c

Map inserts are enlarged sections of Papua, New Guinea, depicting the Papuan Campaign. See Map 18 for geographical correlation.

**e**
INITIAL ADVANCE OF 32ND INFANTRY DIVISION ON BUNA, 16-21 NOV. 1942

**a**
JAPANESE ADVANCE, 21 JULY-16 SEPT. 1942

SCALE IN MILES

**d**
INITIAL ADVANCE OF AUSTRALIAN 7TH DIVISION ON GONA AND THE SANANANDA TRACK, 16-21 NOV. 1942

SCALE IN MILES

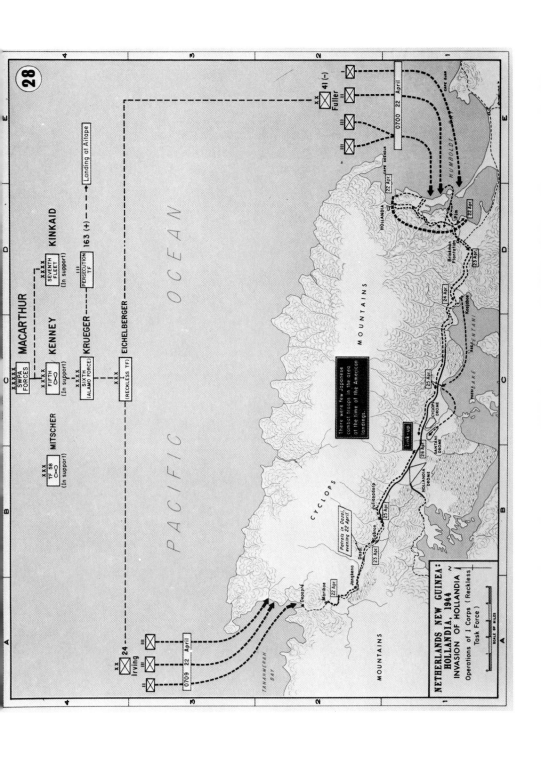

**28**

MACARTHUR

MITSCHER

XXX
TF 58
(In support)

KENNEY

XXXX
FIFTH
FLEET
(In support)

KINKAID

XXXX
SEVENTH
FLEET
(In support)

III
PERSECUTION
TF

163 (+) ----→ Landing at Aitape

KRUEGER

XXXX
SIXTH
(ALAMO FORCE)

EICHELBERGER

XXX
I
(RECKLESS TF)

PACIFIC OCEAN

XX
24
Irving

III

0709  22 April

III

III

TANAHMERAH BAY

MOUNTAINS

Depapré

Maribo  22 Apr

Jangkena

Dazai

23 Apr

Sabron

Julianadorp  25 Apr

Patrols in Dazai
evening 22 April

25 Apr

HOLLANDIA
DROME

SENTANI
DROME

CYCLOPS

26 Apr

Link-up

25 Apr

SENTANI

There were few Japanese
combat troops in the area
at the time of the American
landings.

CYCLOPS DROME

MOUNTAINS

Kojabee

24 Apr

Brinkman
Plantation

23 Apr

HOLLANDIA

22 Apr

Pim

22 Apr

HUMBOLDT

CAPE SOEADJA

CAPE PIE

0700  22 April

III

III

XX
41 (-)
Fuller

NETHERLANDS NEW GUINEA:
HOLLANDIA, 1944
INVASION OF HOLLANDIA
Operations of I Corps (Reckless)
Task Force

SCALE OF MILES

General Douglas MacArthur
(U.S. Army Photo).

Sir Thomas Blamey
(U.S. Army Photo).

General Walter Krueger
(U.S. Army Photo).

Brigadier General Clovis Byers
(U.S. Army Photo).

Infantry of the 41st Division penetrating the jungle at the edge of White Beach, Hollandia, 22 April 1944 (U.S. Army Photo).

Eichelberger in front of world map (U.S. Army Photo).

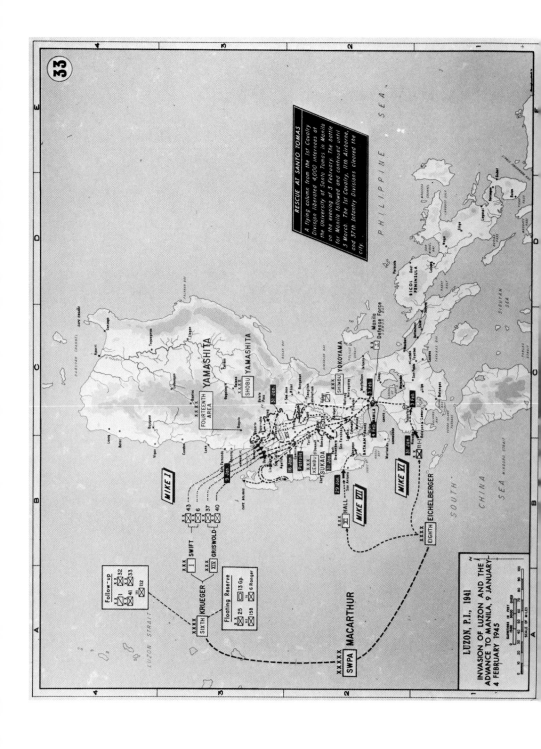

33

**RESCUE AT SANTO TOMAS**

A flying column from the 1st Cavalry Division liberated 4,000 internees at the University of Santo Tomas in Manila on the evening of 3 February. The battle for Manila followed and continued until 3 March. The 1st Cavalry, 11th Airborne, and 37th Infantry Divisions cleared the city.

PHILIPPINE SEA

YAMASHITA

SHOBU YAMASHITA

FOURTEENTH AREA

SHIMBU YOKOYAMA

Manila Defense Force

MIKE I

SWIFT

GRISWOLD

Follow-up

SIXTH KRUEGER

Floating Reserve

SWPA MACARTHUR

MIKE VII

MIKE VI

EIGHTH EICHELBERGER

SOUTH CHINA SEA

**LUZON, P.I., 1941**

INVASION OF LUZON AND THE ADVANCE TO MANILA, 9 JANUARY–4 FEBRUARY 1945

SCALE OF MILES

ELEVATION IN FEET

American officers at the observation post near Cavite, on the road to Manila, Luzon, P.F. *Left to right:* Major General Joseph Swing, Eichelberger, Colonel F. S. Bowen (U.S. Army Photo).

Eichelberger and Filipino guerrillas look at a map on a road 15 miles from Manila (U.S. Army Photo).

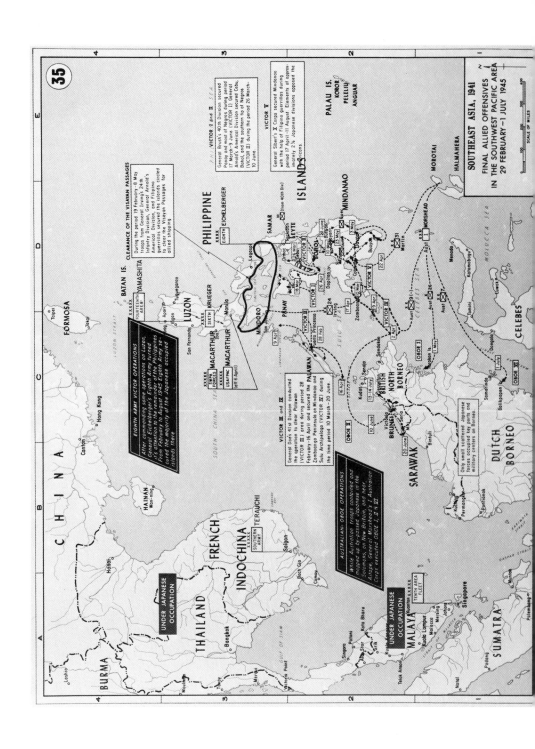

SOUTHEAST ASIA, 1941
FINAL ALLIED OFFENSIVES IN THE SOUTHWEST PACIFIC AREA
29 FEBRUARY–1 JULY 1945

Tanks of the 716th Tank Battalion, Fortieth Division, moving through town on Panay, P.I. (U.S. Army Photo).

General Yamashita, the tiger of Malaya, surrenders to the Thirty-second Division at Kiangun, in northern Luzon (U.S. Army Photo).

General MacArthur talks to reporters on his arrival at Atsugi Airport, Japan (U.S. Army Photo).

Standing in prayer after the first American flag was raised over the American Embassy in Tokyo. *Left to right:* Admiral William Halsey, Eichelberger, and General of the Army Douglas MacArthur (U.S. Army Photo).

use these airfields to conduct bombing missions against Japanese bases in the Philippines, which were only 800 miles away. Since he had expected that the task force would have seized and built up at least one airfield by 10 June, he had promised the Joint Chiefs of Staff that he would support Admiral Chester Nimitz's invasion of Saipan, in the Marianas, on 15 June 1944 with planes from these airfields.[57]

In late May 1944 MacArthur was at the pinnacle of success. He had cut through the Japanese defenses on New Guinea with the skill of a surgeon. The amphibious envelopments at Saidor (2 January), Aitape and Hollandia (22 April), and Wakde (17 May) were outstanding successes. Once Biak was captured, the northern coast of New Guinea would be secured, and MacArthur could commence his long-awaited return to the Philippines.

At 0715 hours on 27 May 1944, Major General Horace Fuller and two regiments (186th and 162nd Infantry) of his Forty-first Division landed at Biak. Although this unit had performed magnificently during the tactical phase of the Hollandia operation, it had not had much opportunity to prepare for this invasion. The Japanese offered no resistance at the beaches, and the initial landings were a complete success. General Fuller's plan called for the 162nd Regiment to move along the beach road, which ran at the base of a steep cliff, to the three airfields. Meanwhile, the 186th Regiment would move on a parallel route through the mountains. In the first two days General Fuller's forces moved quickly, covering eight miles along the beach road, which brought them within 1,000 yards of the first airfield (Mokmer drome).[58]

Unfortunately, MacArthur's Intelligence officer, the pompous General Willoughby, had seriously underestimated the Japanese strength and capability. Instead of the 4,380 Japanese troops that Willoughby had predicted, there were more than 11,000 Japanese soldiers at Biak. These were not the same type troops that the Americans had found at Hollandia. Willoughby had developed an attitude similar to that of Admiral Barbey. He had forgotten the tenacity and ferocity with which the Japanese infantry could conduct a defense. At Biak the Japanese high command had stationed several regiments of superbly trained infantry under the command of Colonel Naoyuki Kuzume, who was "a soldier of the highest calibre and a tactician compelling respect." In addition, Kuzume had had five months to prepare his defenses at Biak.[59]

Colonel Kuzume had astutely assessed the Allied objective as the three airfields along the southern coast of Biak. Therefore he skillfully emplaced his forces in the coral ridges above the coastal road, which ran from Mandom to the Mokmer airfield. He also positioned troops in the compartmented ridge system 1,000 yards north, northwest of the Mokmer airfield. This ridge, composed of numerous caves, completely dominated the coastal road and the three airfields. It provided countless concealed emplacements for the enemy's artillery, mortars, and machine guns.[60]

On 29 May the easy advance of the Forty-first Division toward the airfields suddenly ended. Colonel Kuzume counterattacked with two battalions of infantry, supported by tank and artillery fire, against the 162nd Infantry on the coastal road. In the four-hour fight, the American forces successfully neutralized eight Japanese tanks and destroyed the better part of a Japanese battalion. However, the American advance was stopped cold and the 162nd Infantry prepared defensive positions two miles short of Mokmer airfield, their first objective. General Fuller requested and received the 163rd Infantry Regiment to reinforce his task force. With this additional support, he was able to mount an offensive again and, ten days later, on 8 June, he finally captured his first airfield—Mokmer. However, this was an empty victory because the field was under Japanese gunfire from the dominating ridgeline to the north.[61]

On 14 June 1944 the tactical situation on Biak was bleak. In nineteen days of combat, the Forty-first Division had seized only a single airfield, and that still could not be used by Allied air forces. More important, Admiral Nimitz would have to invade Saipan the next day without the land-based air cover that MacArthur had promised. This failure was noted by the Joint Chiefs of Staff in Washington.[62]

By 14 June 1944, even before the Saipan landing, Biak had become a source of personal embarrassment to MacArthur. In this operation his over-optimistic communiqués backfired on him. He was caught in a blatant lie to the Joint Chiefs of Staff and to the American public.

On 28 May, after General Fuller's initial success, General MacArthur had announced to the American press that the impending fall of Biak "marks the practical end of the New Guinea campaign." On 1 June MacArthur's communiqué proclaimed that Japanese resistance "was collapsing." On 3 June MacArthur's communiqué stated that "mopping up was proceeding on Biak." However, at the same time that MacArthur was announcing to the world this imminent, successful conclusion of the campaign, the Australian press was relaying a totally different story. Spencer Davis reported in the *Australian Newsweek* that "obviously, it would require additional reinforcements to achieve the resounding victory proclaimed ten days ago by General MacArthur."[63]

MacArthur, aware of the discrepancy between the actual tactical situation and his communiqués, became increasingly concerned as time went on. On 5 June he told General Krueger (the Sixth Army commander and General Fuller's immediate supervisor): "I am becoming concerned at the failure to secure the Biak airfields . . . is the advance being pushed with sufficient determination? Our negligible ground losses would seem to indicate a failure to do so." On 14 June an irate MacArthur cabled General Kreuger: "The situation on Biak is unsatisfactory. The strategic purpose of the operation is being jeopardized by the failure to establish without delay an operating field for aircraft."[64]

During the first two weeks of June 1944, as the tactical situation stagnated, MacArthur continued to press General Krueger for results. Krueger, in turn, dispatched a number of radiograms to Fuller urging him to pick up the pace of the advance. But neither MacArthur nor Krueger ever saw fit to go to Biak to see firsthand what the situation was like. Krueger, in a move reminiscent of MacArthur at Buna, sent staff officers to observe the fighting and report on the delay. Colonel Kenneth Sweany, the chief of staff of the Forty-first Division, recalled that Colonel Clyde Eddleman, the Sixth Army operations officer and a confidant of General Krueger, "saw only what could be seen from the beach, couldn't have the vaguest notion of this hellish terrain, and brought back to Krueger . . . God knows what he brought back." As at Buna, the blame for the poor situation at Biak was attributed to a lack of determination at the company and battalion levels. Sweany, who was a close personal friend of General Fuller, resented the insinuations by Krueger's staff and the insulting telegrams sent to Fuller. Sweany believed that the Sixth Army commander and his staff failed to show the Forty-first Division any loyalty.[65]

With the tactical situation stalemated, victory having been proclaimed two weeks earlier and the invasion of Saipan scheduled for the next day, MacArthur and Krueger called for their most able field commander to salvage the situation and put out this fire before it consumed their reputations. At 1800 hours, on 14 June 1944, Krueger summoned General Eichelberger to an emergency conference at his headquarters. Krueger was a hard-nosed and demanding officer. He was born in Germany and had enlisted in the American army as a private in the Spanish-American War. In the following forty-six years, he had fought his way through the ranks by raw talent to command the Sixth Army. Although a consummate professional, Krueger could be harsh and insensitive in dealing with subordinates. He lacked people skills. At this meeting Eichelberger, whose sole responsibility had been the build-up at Hollandia, was briefed for the first time about the situation at Biak. Krueger told Eichelberger that the continuous fighting, difficult terrain, and intense heat had seriously affected the aggressiveness and determination of the American infantry. Krueger instructed Eichelberger to take command the following morning.[66]

At 0830 hours on 15 June, Eichelberger and a small staff of trusted assistants departed for Biak. They arrived at General Fuller's headquarters at 1230 hours. Krueger's plan had been to insert Eichelberger at a new level—task force commander—between himself and Fuller, who would remain as division commander. However, Fuller, insulted by the tone of the Sixth Army radiograms, felt that Krueger had lost confidence in him. He requested that MacArthur relieve him. Eichelberger's first task was to try and dissuade Fuller from taking this action. Unfortunately, the feisty Fuller was adamant and Eichelberger had to conduct the campaign without him. Eichelberger then appointed Brigadier General Jens Doe, who had been so effective at Sanananda, as the new division commander.[67] General Doe, the big, burly son of a Norwegian immigrant, was to prove a superb division commander and a great help to Eichelberger in the days to come.

Eichelberger spent the first two-and-one-half days at the front familiarizing himself with the tactical situation and the fighting capabilities of his own forces. On 16 June he went to the regimental command posts of the 186th and 162nd Infantry regiments to assess personally the morale and effectiveness of those units. On 17 June he observed the conduct of the two units under fire. Eichelberger radioed General Krueger: "Today I have been with General Doe and 186 and 162 Infantry. With the possible exception of the first Bn 162

Inf the troops are not nearly as exhausted as I had expected and I believe they can be made to fight with energy."[68]

On 17 June General Krueger, still under pressure from MacArthur, radioed Eichelberger to "Launch your attack . . . promptly and press it home with the utmost vigor." Eichelberger, however, had been in this situation before. He had a plan for defeating the Japanese and was not going to be rushed because MacArthur and Krueger were embarrassed by previous communiqués. On 17 June Eichelberger sent a succint message to General Krueger:

> Having arrived here forty-eight hours ago in almost complete ignorance of the situation, I have spent two days at the front. Tomorrow [Sunday], I have called off all fighting and troops will be reorganized. On Monday, I propose to put three battalions in the rear of the Japanese, and on Tuesday I propose to take the other two airfields.[69]

After informing Krueger of his plan and his pace, Eichelberger took two additional actions on 17 June. First, he ordered a reinforced rifle company to occupy Hill 320, which was the dominating terrain feature in the area north of the three airfields, thus providing an excellent observation point. Second, Eichelberger issued his instructions for the 19 June attack. Eichelberger believed that the problem at Biak was not training or leadership, but tactics. To assault frontally the Japanese positions on the ridge above the airfields would be suicide. This tactical dilemma had stymied the Forty-first Division for three weeks. Eichelberger had been in a similar situation at Buna. He knew the heavy cost in human lives of a frontal attack. His creative mind was always seeking new solutions to difficult problems and at Biak he was willing to innovate. He would not try to seize the airfields directly or to conduct a frontal attack against the Japanese positions. Instead, he would envelop the enemy by going around their southern flank and seizing the ridgeline north of Mokmer airfield from the rear. Eichelberger's objectives were to eliminate the Japanese ability to fire on Mokmer airfield and to obtain favorable terrain from which to launch future advances.[70]

Eichelberger later credited the Japanese with giving him the solution for cracking their defenses. He had carefully examined all their operations in World War II and believed that the Japanese tactics in Malaya would provide the method of ending the stalemate on Biak.

In Malaya, each time the British forces prepared a defensive line, the Japanese enveloped it. Once the British discovered that the Japanese were in their rear, the whole defensive line collapsed and the British withdrew to establish another. This process had been repeated down the entire peninsula. Eichelberger believed that at Biak the "Japanese troops [would], just like occidental troops, take a very dim and unhappy view of enemy forces in their rear."[71]

On 18 June Eichelberger repeated a lesson he had learned at Buna and rested his troops before the major attack. As the soldiers rested, Eichelberger gave his subordinate commanders time to reorganize their forces and to ensure that "Everybody could find out what they were doing." Eichelberger also sent out patrols to reconnoiter the Japanese positions, and by evening on 18 June his troops were, in the words of an eyewitness, "ready to move hard and fast."[72]

On the morning of 19 June, Eichelberger launched his attack. The highly trained soldiers of the Forty-first Division moved hard and fast to accomplish Eichelberger's innovative battle plan. The Japanese headquarters was in what Eichelberger called "the sump." This had been a huge cave whose roof had collapsed. Now it was a huge hole in the ground. There were numerous caves connected to this large depression, from which the Japanese could fire on the airstrip and then hide. Knowing a frontal attack was suicide, Eichelberger had three battalions move around the rear and seize the high ground behind the sump. Once he occupied this position, the Japanese in the caves and sump were isolated and cut off from all reinforcement or escape. With the Japanese holed up in their caves, the Mokmer airfield could finally be used by American planes.[73]

Although the attack on 19 June was an overwhelming success, the battle was not yet over. The original mission of the Forty-first Division was to seize three airfields, not one. To accomplish this, Eichelberger attacked the following morning and captured the other two airfields. The remaining Japanese in the region were holed up in the west caves. Eichelberger had a healthy respect for the tenacity and determination of the Japanese soldier. He knew that the campaign would not be over until this last pocket of resistance had been eliminated. He continued to press the attack.[74]

On the night of 21–22 June, Colonel Kuzume recognized defeat. He destroyed his regimental colors and all official documents and then ordered all able-bodied soldiers to attempt a breakout. The Japanese tried three times to break through the lines of the Forty-first Division. At 2100 hours, and then at 2400 hours on 21 June, the Japanese attacked and were repulsed by the Americans. At 0400 hours on 22 June the Japanese tried for the final time. All three attacks failed. The last Japanese resistance in the caves was finally mopped up on 27 June.

Eichelberger departed Biak to return to Hollandia on 28 June 1944. His reputation as the Fireman of the Southwest Pacific had been confirmed. It had taken him only five days to seize the three Japanese airfields and to break the enemy's main line of defense. At a cost of 400 American lives, 4,700 Japanese had been killed. With Biak secured, MacArthur could move on to his cherished operations in the Philippines.[75]

Eichelberger received very little publicity for his accomplishments. However, there was a marked change in the attitude toward him of MacArthur and his staff. MacArthur realized that his reputation and personal integrity were on the line at Biak. He recognized that Eichelberger had solved the tactical situation so quickly that his—MacArthur's—reputation had not been tarnished. MacArthur had been a professional soldier for forty-three years and he knew that Eichelberger had to be rewarded for his stellar performance at Hollandia and Biak. MacArthur decided to grant Eichelberger his most cherished desire—the command of an army. Shortly after Eichelberger returned to Hollandia, he was appointed the commanding general of the new Eighth United States Army.

Thus, eighteen months after Buna, Eichelberger was finally an army commander. Three of his classmates from West Point had already received this honor: George Patton had the Third Army and was about to become the most famous American army commander of World War II; William Simpson had the Ninth Army; and Jacob Devers, the senior man in that class, had the Sixth Army Group. (An Army Group was responsible for coordinating two or more armies.) In 1944 no corps commander in the United States Army had seen more combat than had Eichelberger. He had earned his army command in some of the toughest fighting of the war.

As a corps commander, Eichelberger had no peer. He had learned a great deal from the Japanese at Buna. At Hollandia and at Biak he avenged that experience. Eichelberger had been determined, after Buna, that the next time he went into battle the Japanese would have to worry about facing veteran American soldiers. He had wanted them to know fear. And at Hollandia, and again at Biak, they had.

At Buna, Eichelberger had learned the importance of a realistic training program, innovative tactics, and dynamic personal leadership. At Hollandia his superbly conditioned and highly trained soldiers disrupted the Japanese defenses and moved so rapidly that the enemy was never able to recover. This campaign was successful because of the flexibility and initiative displayed by subordinate officers. His officers had gone to the most critical locations on the battlefield and were able to make quick decisions and maintain the tempo of the attack.

At Biak he again utilized highly trained American soldiers. However, in this battle the key to success was tactics. Eichelberger was a knowledgeable and experienced officer who was also very creative and able to discern new solutions to difficult problems. He refused to let his way of thinking become rigid or to execute a bloody frontal attack. Instead, he executed a daring and complex envelopment which completely destroyed the Japanese defenses.

As a corp commander Eichelberger repaid the Japanese for the lessons they had taught him at Buna. He also remained MacArthur's "Fireman." As an army commander he would prove conclusively to the Japanese, and to Douglas MacArthur, that he was the finest field commander of the war—even though he was the least known.

# · 4 ·

# The Payoff in the Philippines

EICHELBERGER WOULD BECOME THE MOST SUCCESSFUL GENERAL IN
the United States Army. His troops would capture more enemy-
held territory, in less time, than those of any other general of
World War II. MacArthur took the credit, but Eichelberger did
the dirty work. Had he been in the European Theater, Britain's
Viscount Montgomery probably would have envied him more than
Patton.

Eichelberger was a winner. He knew how to beat the Japanese,
even when he was outmanned and outgunned. He moved with cun-
ning and speed. The Japanese were always off balance. Because of
his repeated victories in the Pacific, many of which saved MacArthur's reputation, Eichelberger finally received the greatest honor a
soldier of his rank could expect: command of the newly formed
Eighth Army. And the Eighth Army punished the Japanese.

Had the war lasted, MacArthur had decided that the Eighth
Army under Eichelberger would spearhead the invasion of the Japanese mainland. Not Krueger, or Eisenhower, or Patton, or Bradley.
But Eichelberger. He was the master of the amphibious landing. The
rapid-strike advocate.

But nothing came easily for Eichelberger. Neither MacArthur nor
Krueger took it upon himself to tell the man that he had been chosen
to head the new army. He never knew why they acted so mysteri-

ously, why he had to find out by accident of his appointment. The memory of this callousness of his superiors never left Eichelberger.

To a professional soldier, command of an army was the epitome of a career. It meant that his superiors had recognized his skills as being far above average. He was a leader. He had arrived at the top of his profession.[1] To command an army was equivalent to running a major corporation, except that one's "employees" could be wounded or killed. The logistics were mind-boggling, the challenges blood-curdling, the results history-making. Eichelberger never flinched.

An army commander was responsible for two or more corps on a battlefield. He was a high-level manager in combat, and thousands of lives depended on how he conducted his units under battle conditions. Eichelberger was one of the best field commanders the United States had in World War II. The problem was that he was not appreciated by some of his superiors, including MacArthur. Krueger was jealous of him, and he treated Eichelberger poorly.

In the summer of 1944 the Japanese were still a formidable enemy. Their performance at Biak had proved that. Eichelberger understood the facts of life. He knew that the closer the Americans got to the Japanese mainland, the more vicious and brutal the Japanese resistance would become. As an army commander he could not afford to relax. The lives of thousands of American soldiers were his responsibility and he had to make sure they were prepared for battle.

The campaigns to come—the Philippines and the islands of Japan itself—would be the most difficult of his career. He worried about the casualties and fretted about the challenges that he would have to live with as a battlefield commander. But he never lost confidence. He sensed victory.

Eichelberger knew he would have to drive himself, his subordinates, his troops harder than ever before, because the stakes were total victory. Anything less would be failure. Eichelberger also understood that despite the American victories on New Guinea and elsewhere, the Japanese were far from a defeated, disorganized army. They were dangerous and aggressive. But they had underestimated him. He remembered Buna, and they would pay for that lesson in total defeat.

Eichelberger made the Eighth Army a deadly fighting force. He and his commanders honed it into the most successful force of World War II; he put his personal stamp on the army's performance. They were ready for combat; they knew what to expect! He would never again lead American soldiers into combat unprepared for the rigors, challenges, and surprises of warfare. He would be so successful in the battles to come that MacArthur would proclaim at war's end that "no army of this war has achieved greater glory and distinction than the Eighth."[2]

Late in the afternoon of 30 June 1944, Eichelberger paid a social visit to his old friend Major General Frederick Irving, whose Twenty-fourth Division was still stationed in Hollandia. Eichelberger expected to have a drink or two and some conversation with one of his favorite division commanders.

Upon his arrival at Irving's headquarters, Eichelberger was surprised to find Brigadier General Robert Shoe, the acting chief of staff of the Eighth Army, there. Shoe was a low-key, straightforward officer. Shoe puzzled Eichelberger by asking where he should locate Eighth Army headquarters. Shoe had only thirty-six men with him at the moment, but he expected 1,800 more within the month. Eichelberger, who had not known that another army was assigned to the theater, asked Shoe who the commander was. Shoe then told Eichelberger that *he* was the new commander. Shoe said MacArthur had personally informed him of Eichelberger's selection. Eichelberger was naturally overwhelmed by this news. Unfortunately, he could not obtain verification of Shoe's statement for almost a month. It was not until 28 July that Krueger finally admitted to Eichelberger that it was official; he was the Eighth Army commander. Eichelberger not unnaturally strongly resented Krueger's secretiveness. he felt that after Hollandia and Biak, Krueger owed him a little more respect. As a rival army commander, Eichelberger was now in a position to outshine his former boss.[3]

The Eighth Army staff that arrived at Hollandia consisted of 600 officers and 1,200 enlisted men. This was the brain of a field army, the administrative, logistical, and planning sections. Eichelberger immediately moved the I Corps, which was due to deploy forward with the Sixth Army, out of its quarters and had the new Eighth Army enlarge the quarters and move in.

Giving up command of I Corps was very difficult for Eichelberger. He had formed an extremely close bond with his staff. In the brutal fighting at Buna, Hollandia, and Biak, they had performed brilliantly. For someone as personally involved and as sensitive as Eichelberger, this separation was painful. However, the blow was softened by the fact that he was turning over his beloved corps to a close personal friend—Major General Innis Palmer Swift. Swift had been the commander of the First Cavalry Division, which was a superbly trained unit. General Krueger had been very much impressed by Swift's conduct of several independent actions and endorsed his elevation to corps commander. Eichelberger, who knew Swift to be an outstanding soldier, strongly concurred.[4]

As the new Eighth Army staff set about the task of enlarging quarters and moving in at Hollandia, Eichelberger was quickly impressed by their professionalism and efficiency. The staff had previously been the staff of the Second Army stationed at Memphis, Tennessee, a staff handpicked and trained by Lieutenant General Ben Lear before he moved up to be the head of Army Ground Forces in Washington. Lear's toughness and ability to enforce high standards in the army were legendary. He did not suffer fools lightly, and George C. Marshall described him as "loyal, stern and drastic." He did not like yes men. He would accept on his staff only soldiers who were capable of imagination and independent thought while also capable of attention to detail. Eichelberger was always intensely grateful to Lear for the "outstanding group" he had given to him.[5]

Eichelberger, unlike MacArthur, relied heavily on his staff. MacArthur did not have a close personal relationship with anyone. However, he was intensely loyal to his staff. Krueger believed that this loyalty was misplaced, because it led him to overlook many of their faults and mistakes. Unfortunately, the rigidity of thinking and ineptness of MacArthur's staff caused a number of problems and hard feelings in the theater. Eichelberger, on the other hand, surrounded himself with young, dynamic officers capable of flexible and innovative thinking. Because of the demands Eichelberger placed on his staff in combat, he usually sought younger men because their physical stamina allowed them to operate without sleep for long periods of time.

Eichelberger's Eighth Army staff was a unique blend of proven, trusted assistants and new, talented officers. He enhanced the staff he had inherited from General Lear by including several of his best subordinates from I Corps. He brought his most trusted confidant, Brigadier General Clovis Byers, to be his chief of staff, and the youthful Colonel Frank Bowen to be his operations officer. Both were combat veterans who had been with Eichelberger at Buna.

They had shared his experiences in that harsh crucible of battle and they were the most ardent supporters of his training program. They also emphasized the importance of innovative and flexible tactics. Bowen, as the planner of all Eichelberger's operations, would never recommend a frontal assault. They were both imbued with Eichelberger's philosophy of leadership by example. By the summer of 1944 Byers had earned the Distinguished Service Cross, Silver Star, Purple Heart, and two Bronze Star medals. At the same time, Bowen had the Distinguished Service Cross, two Silver Stars, and a Bronze Star medal.[6]

Byers and Bowen served on Eichelberger's staff throughout the war. This was a distinct asset to Eichelberger because their combat experience complemented the enthusiasm and professionalism of the rest of his new staff. Eichelberger believed that it was an advantage to have a staff composed of officers newly assigned to the theater because, "having come freshly from home they were not haunted with the desire for rotation and other things which come up after officers have been out here for 18 months." It should be noted that, by serving with Eichelberger throughout the war, Byers and Bowen put their personal careers in jeopardy. Promotion in the army is based on successful command in the field. Many of their contemporaries were commanding regiments or divisions and they ran the risk of being overlooked for future promotion. However, they never had to worry about their careers. Eichelberger was an intensely loyal individual and constantly fought for their recognition and promotion throughout the war. After the war he served as their mentor and most ardent supporter. They both went on to distinguished careers and retired as lieutenant generals.[7]

Throughout August 1944, as the staff of the Eighth Army was impressing Eichelberger with its professionalism and efficiency, he was having a similar effect on them. Colonel John Jannarone, the assistant Eighth Army engineer, was encouraged by Eichelberger's personal attention to, grandfather-like treatment of, the new staff. Jannarone was in an excellent position to assess Eichelberger's leadership style and to evaluate his relationship with the new staff. At age thirty Jannarone was already a marked man in the Corps of Engineers. He had been a star football, basketball, and baseball player at West Point as well as the number-one student in academics. He was tough, hard, and aggressive. Jannarone was very much involved in the construction of the new Eighth Army headquarters.

During this work he found that Eichelberger always made a point of observing this arduous labor and talking to the soldiers. He had a unique common touch in dealing with subordinates. On one occasion Eichelberger gave Jannarone an ice-cold glass of lemonade. Forty years later Jannarone described with great glee how much it hit the spot. Eichelberger treated his staff with kindness and respect and they responded with exceptional loyalty and dedication.[8]

Although Eichelberger closely supervised every aspect of the Eighth Army's deployment to New Guinea, it was not until late August 1944 that he was finally relieved of his responsibilities as the I Corps commander. He did not formally take command of the Eighth Army until 7 September 1944.

In the fall of that year, the premier fighting organization in the Southwest Pacific was Krueger's Sixth Army. Their mission was to prepare for MacArthur's most cherished dream—the invasion of the Philippines. MacArthur believed that the Philippines were the key to victory in the Pacific. The archipelago lay directly across the sea routes between Japan and its vital raw materials in the Dutch East Indies, Malaya, and Indochina. MacArthur's strategic objective was to seize air and sea bases in the Philippines. Once he had done this, he could cut the flow of these raw materials to the Japanese mainland. Thus their war resources would soon be depleted and they would no longer be able to maintain their formidable war machine. This, he reasoned, would bring an end to the war.[9]

In order for the Sixth Army to prepare for this invasion and subsequent reconquest of the Philippines, the Eighth Army had to assume control of all other operational areas in the theater. This meant "mopping up" Japanese resistance on New Guinea, New Britain, and in the Admiralty Islands. It also administered and provided logistical support to more than 200,000 soldiers dispersed over twenty separate locations. Finally, the Eighth Army was ordered to provide the Sixth Army with any training or logistical support it desired. It was difficult for Eichelberger to motivate his staff and soldiers for this support role when they all desired to participate in the glamorous invasions to be conducted by the Sixth Army. However, he never complained and his soldiers performed these missions with great aplomb.[10]

Despite the administrative complexity of coordinating the operations of 200,000 troops in twenty locations, Eichelberger refused to allow his soldiers to think of themselves as support troops. He immediately initiated a vigorous training program for the combat troops in the Eighth Army in order to prepare them for the bitter fighting he anticipated that they would encounter in the Philippines. Eichelberger used the same philosophy and program for training the Eighth Army that had proved so successful with the I Corps. As an army commander he was still haunted by the specter of Buna. He was determined that the Japanese forces who encountered the Eighth Army would be demoralized by the physical toughness and tactical dexterity of the Americans.[11]

Throughout all Eighth Army training exercises, Eichelberger again sought to inculcate responsibility, self-reliance, and initiative in his noncommissioned officers and junior officers. He wanted to develop leaders who were capable of acting on their own when the occasion demanded, and motivating their soldiers to accomplish the most difficult and hazardous of missions. He needed small-unit leaders capable of conducting independent operations without continuous supervision from higher authorities. Eichelberger's emphasis on the development of small-unit leadership proved decisive between November 1944 and May 1945, when thirty-five of the fifty-one amphibious assaults conducted by the Eighth Army were executed by units that were battalion-sized or smaller.[12]

After two months of intensive training, Eichelberger was given the opportunity to test the results of his training program in combat. On 15 and 19 November 1944, the Eighth Army launched two amphibious operations against the Asia and Mapia atolls off the coast of New Guinea. These atolls were needed for naval bases. Both operations were overwhelming successes. The landing at the Asia atoll was not opposed by the Japanese. At the Mapia atoll, Eichelberger landed a single infantry battalion. This small unit moved so fast that it captured the island, killing 159 Japanese at a cost of only twelve Americans. This was an excellent portent of the performance of the Eighth Army in future operations.[13]

Throughout the early fall of 1944, as Eichelberger prepared the Eighth Army for combat, General MacArthur fine-tuned his plans for the invasion of the Philippines, using the Sixth Army. There are three major island groups in the Philippines: Luzon and the adjacent islands in the northern sector; the Visayan Islands, which include Samar and Leyte in the central sector; Mindanao and the Sulu Archipelago in the south. MacArthur's main objective in the Philippines was Luzon, which was its largest island. Once this island was seized, the vital flow of resources and raw materials to Japan from the Dutch East Indies, Malaya, and Indochina would be cut. In addition, MacArthur could use the airfields and naval facilities on Luzon for his offensive against the Japanese mainland. MacArthur selected Leyte as the entrance point into the Philippines. He believed that this island could be captured quickly and then rapidly built up into a major air and supply base, which would support the invasion of Luzon.[14]

On 20 October 1944 the invasion of the Philippines began, when the Sixth Army landed on the eastern coast of Leyte Island. This was the largest invasion conducted by MacArthur up to that time. Two full corps landed on Leyte—the X Corps, which was composed of the First Cavalry and the Twenty-fourth Division; and the XXIV Corps, consisting of the Seventh and Ninety-sixth divisions. Together these two assault forces contained 104,000 men. General Willoughby, MacArthur's ever inaccurate Intelligence officer, estimated that the Japanese had only 21,000 soldiers to oppose this landing on Leyte. In reality, there were 35,000 Japanese soldiers on Leyte. Willoughby's estimate would not have been so bad if he had anticipated that the Japanese would reinforce Leyte. Unfortunately, Willoughby lacked the independence of thought to deduce accurately the Japanese reactions.

General Yamashita was the commander of all Japanese ground forces in the Philippines. He was a short, muscular, bald-headed legend to the soldiers in his own army as a result of his dramatic victory at Malaya. Yamashita desired to fight a decisive battle in the Philippines on Luzon. However, his superior, Field Marshal Hisaichi Terauchi, overruled him and ordered Leyte reinforced. As a result the Japanese garrison on Leyte was increased to 80,000. This impressive force fought with great skill and tenacity. They made excellent use of the terrain in their defense and they gave up ground only after bitter and bloody fighting. They proved conclusively on Leyte that their morale and fighting spirit had not yet been broken. They were as stubborn in giving up ground on Leyte as they had been in New Guinea.

After sixty-seven bitter days of combat, from 20 October to 26 December 1944, the Sixth Army had killed 55,344 Japanese, but the island was still not completely secured. The Sixth Army Intelligence officer claimed that Japanese resistance had been broken and that only 5,000 enemy soldiers were left of the island. On 26 December MacArthur issued another communiqué, which claimed that the Leyte campaign was concluded except for "minor mopping-up."[15]

This communiqué did not tell the real story of Leyte. The skillful defense of the Japanese had disrupted MacArthur's timetable for future operations in the Philippines. His projected invasion of Luzon had been postponed from 20 December 1944 to 9 January 1945. Eichelberger took a perverse sense of satisfaction out of Krueger's difficulties on Leyte. He told his wife that Krueger would "have to pull his hand out of his shirt front" because he did "not qualify as Napoleon." In order for the Sixth Army to conduct the invasion of Luzon, MacArthur gave Eichelberger and the Eighth Army the mission of completing the Leyte campaign. Eichelberger knew his boss well and had anticipated MacArthur's onerous communiqué, in a letter to his wife. He told her that when he took over on Leyte he hoped that "nobody insults my intelligence by making the task an illegitimate child known as 'mopping-up.' The only difference between a big fight and mopping-up is that when victory is obtained, nobody will call it that. It is just as difficult and the bullets go by just as fast."[16]

When the Eighth Army took control of the tactical situation on Leyte, Eichelberger soon discovered that his worst fears were a reality. The Japanese army was still very much intact and was still capable of extremely stubborn resistance. He found that MacArthur had prematurely declared the island secure as soon as two divisions had broken through the Japanese positions to the west coast of the island. In the four-month period, from 26 December 1944 to 8 May 1945, the Eighth Army was engaged in some of the most demanding and brutal fighting of the entire Pacific war. In this time Eichelberger's soldiers would kill 24,294 soldiers. This was five times the number that MacArthur's Intelligence officer stated were left on the island.[17]

Eichelberger's distaste for the term "mopping up" should not be understood as personal vanity or egotism. He was outraged at the term for morale and moral reasons, not because it affected the publicity of his campaigns. He found it difficult to keep his soldiers at the razor's edge of combat readiness when they had already been told that the fight was over. He also believed that it was not a good enough phrase to ask men to die for. In fact, he was so intensely outraged at the dichotomy between MacArthur's optimistic communiqué and the brutality of the fighting on Leyte that he risked his career and spoke to the press. He contradicted MacArthur and told reporters that Leyte contained "the greatest reservoir of Japanese in the Philippines."[18]

Although Eichelberger was irritated by MacArthur's description of the fighting on Leyte, it did not affect his performance. He accomplished his mission of destroying all Japanese strongholds on the island with a great deal of perseverance and professional skill. The Japanese tactics on Leyte were designed to be bloody and time-consuming for the Americans. They offered stubborn resistance until their defensive positions were broken and then they withdrew in small groups to new defensive positions. With each subsequent withdrawal, Japanese resistance became increasingly dispersed and isolated. Eichelberger's emphasis on small-unit training, especially patrolling, proved to be the key to his success on Leyte against such tactics. Once he had disrupted the initial Japanese defenses, the aggressive patrolling of his troops frustrated any attempt by the Japanese to reorganize a defense.[19]

As an army commander, Eichelberger had responsibilities in addition to the tactical operations on Leyte. The Eighth Army was also responsible for providing logistical support to the two corps on Leyte. This meant ensuring an uninterrupted flow of fighting men and supplies to the combat zone. A system for providing fuel for wheeled and tracked vehicles and the engineers' heavy equipment had to be established, damaged equipment had to be recovered and repaired, and in addition Eichelberger was expected to provide the same service to all units that were designated to reinforce the Sixth Army on Luzon. This proved to be an immense undertaking because these forces were spread out in nineteen separate locations in Australia, New Guinea, the Admiralties, New Britain, Morotai, and the Philippines. Eichelberger's dynamic and hardworking staff handled this demanding task flawlessly.[20]

In addition to these two major duties, Eichelberger and his staff had to plan and prepare for their own future operations, which included amphibious landings to reconquer Mindoro, Palawan, and Zamboanga and the clearing of the Visayan passages.

Although he was faced with a myriad of complex operations and responsibilities, Eichelberger did not allow himself to become isolated from his soldiers. He realized that victory depended on the morale, courage, and esprit of the individual soldier. He had an excellent understanding of human nature and a thorough grasp of the needs and desires of his men. It was not a put-on phony concern; Eichelberger really loved talking and interacting with his enlisted men. On 1 January 1945 Eichelberger went forward to the Seventy-seventh Division headquarters on Leyte and awarded more than a hundred medals for heroism in action. As he presented these decorations, he made a point of spending some time talking to each soldier. He believed that these medals were an important motivational factor because they physically recognized the soldier's achievement. Despite MacArthur's stingy attitude toward decorations, Eichelberger was adamant in ensuring that his soldiers were quickly and justly rewarded for their heroism. In the month of January 1945 alone, Eichelberger conducted five such award ceremonies.

On 2 January 1945 Eichelberger displayed another example of his consideration and concern for his men. He went to a field hospital on Leyte to visit his wounded soldiers. At first glance, this would not seem unique. All leaders who really care about their troops should visit them in the hospital. However, Eichelberger had a unique empathy for his soldiers and did not show up empty-handed. He brought ice cream packed in ice to his traumatized soldiers that day. The young wounded men, who were suffering in the intense heat on Leyte, were deeply touched by Eichelberger's kindness. They quickly ate the ice cream and then made ice water from the ice it was packed in.[21]

Throughout January 1945, as Eichelberger aggressively pursued the Japanese forces on Leyte, Krueger and the Sixth Army commenced the decisive battle in the Philippines—the invasion of Luzon. This landing tool place at Lingayen Gulf on 9 January 1945. General Willoughby erred again. He estimated that there were only 150,000 Japanese forces on Luzon. General Krueger called this figure a "very considerable underestimate"; in reality the Japanese had 275,000 men on Luzon. These troops were commanded by the best field commander in the Japanese army—Yamashita, the Tiger of Malaya. Yamashita believed that he did not have enough troops to defend the entire island. He reasoned that his forces would not be sufficient to hold the Manila Bay region against the massive assault that MacArthur would launch against him. Yamashita's plan for the defense of Luzon, therefore, did not include a withdrawal into the

Bataan Peninsula as MacArthur had done in 1941–42. He believed that MacArthur would be able to isolate and rapidly overwhelm him in this narrow peninsula. Instead, Yamashita planned to concentrate his forces in the mountainous strongholds of northern Luzon. From there he could delay the Allied invasion of his homeland for at least a year by monopolizing a large quantity of American ground troops, aircraft, and naval assets. It would be a time-consuming process for MacArthur to root the Japanese out of their mountain defenses and it would be very costly in American lives.[22]

In order to accomplish this strategy, Yamashita divided his forces on Luzon into regional defense zones. The largest force, known as the Shobo Group, consisted of 152,000 men under Yamashita's personal control. Yamashita anticipated that MacArthur would invade Luzon at Lingayen Gulf, but decided he would not contest this landing. Instead he would threaten the left flank of the Sixth Army as they advanced the 120 miles from Lingayen Gulf to Manila. This group had the primary responsibility of conducting the protracted defense in the rugged mountains of northern Luzon.

The second (central) defensive force was the Kembu Group, which consisted of 30,000 men under the command of Major General Rikichi Tsukada. This small group had two missions: first, it was to deny the Americans the use of Clark Field, which was the best air base on Luzon, for as long as possible; then it would conduct delaying operations in the Zambales Mountains west of the airfield and on the right flank of the Sixth Army drive to Manila, for as long as possible. The third (southern) defensive force was the Shimbu Group, which was composed of 80,000 men under the command of Lieutenant General Shizuo Yokoyama. This unit was responsible for the defense of southern Luzon. However, this defense did not include the city of Manila. Yamashita instructed Yokoyama to withdraw into the mountains east of the city and to cut off the city's water supply from the reservoirs. He was also to delay the American advance for as long as possible. Unfortunately for the city of Manila, this order was not obeyed. As a result of a bureaucratic dispute between the Japanese army and navy, Admiral Iwabuchi refused to obey the order of General Yokoyama. Iwabuchi directed the navy and marine forces in Manila to remain and to defend Japanese naval facilities.[23]

On 9 January 1945 General Krueger and the Sixth Army landed on the southern coast of the Lingayen Gulf. The assault troops for this operation consisted of Eichelberger's former command, I Corps, and the XIV Corps which included the Fortieth, Thirty-seventh, Sixth, and Forty-third divisions. As a result of Yamashita's strategy, there was little opposition to Krueger's landing or his initial advance. However, the pace of Krueger's southward drive toward Manila was slow. Krueger felt that his logistical lifeline needed to be established on Luzon to support his 200,000 soldiers. Airstrips had to be built, roads fixed, and bridges (which the Japanese had destroyed) reconstructed. Krueger also had to be careful because Yamashita had placed powerful forces in the mountains on both flanks of his drive on Manila.[24]

MacArthur's plan for the reconquest of the Philippines did not envision a slow, methodical advance to Manila. MacArthur's pride had been seriously hurt by his defeat in the Philippines in 1941. In order to avenge this loss and to humiliate the Japanese, MacArthur wanted to defeat them quickly. He very much desired to celebrate his sixty-fifth birthday, on 26 January 1945, in Manila. On 12 January, just three days after the Lingayen landing, MacArthur summoned Krueger to his headquarters to complain of the slow progress of the Sixth Army. MacArthur demanded that Krueger pick up the pace of his advance. MacArthur used the same arguments with Krueger that he had with Eichelberger at Buna: losses had been low, therefore resistance must be light. He told Krueger that Yamashita would not defend Manila and would declare it an open city as MacArthur had in 1942. Krueger protested that the pace of the advance could not be picked up but stated that MacArthur "did not seem impressed by my arguments."[25]

Throughout the month of January 1945 the occupation of Manila became an obsession with MacArthur, and the slow progress of the Sixth Army a great irritant. On 23 January Eichelberger was informed that Krueger had been given an ultimatum by MacArthur to be in Manila by 5 February. When even this date looked doubtful and MacArthur's birthday had come and gone, he personally went to the front to investigate the reason for the Sixth Army's slow advance. MacArthur was not pleased by what he saw. He found the pace "much too leisurely." He emphatically told General Krueger that he had observed "a noticeable lack of drive and aggressive initiative" in the Thirty-seventh Division. In anger and frustration MacArthur bluntly told Eichelberger that the Sixth Army was "mentally incapable" of a rapid advance; but, he added, if he gave them overwhelming force, they could "advance ponderously and slowly to victory."[26]

After three years of bitter fighting against the Japanese, MacArthur knew whom to call on when he wanted results. If Krueger and the Sixth Army would not capture Manila for him, then he would send in his Fireman to solve this problem on Luzon. MacArthur directed Eichelberger to conduct two amphibious landings on Luzon, one to the west and one to the south of Manila.

The first landing took place on 29 January when Eichelberger landed the XI Corps, under the command of Major General Charles P. (Chink) Hall at Subic Bay. The assault troops for this operation were the Thirty-eighth Infantry Division and the Thirty-fourth Regimental Combat Team. This landing force at Subic Bay had three important missions: (1) they were to seal off the Bataan Peninsula so that the Japanese could not use it to deny the Americans the use of Manila Bay, as MacArthur had done in 1941–42, (2) they were to secure a beachhead and to open Subic Bay for American shipping; (3) they were to capture the fighter airstrip, which was located at San Marcelino, rapidly.[27]

Although these missions were difficult for such a small assault force, Eichelberger had a great deal of confidence in the XI Corps commander. Major General Charles Hall, at age fifty-nine, was a dynamic and inspirational troop commander. In World War I Hall had established an enviable reputation for courageous leadership, while earning a Distinguished Service Cross and three Silver Stars. He was the type of officer who cared about his men and led by example. The Distinguished Service Cross he received in World War I was awarded for advancing through heavy machine-gun fire to rescue one of his wounded men. At the outset of World War II he organized the Ninety-third Division, which was the nation's first all-black division. This unit performed in a superior manner in the Pacific in World War II.

The XI Corps landed on Luzon at 0830 hours on 29 January 1945. Eichelberger's demanding training program and Chink Hall's inspirational leadership paid handsome dividends. The unit pushed forward twelve miles in the first three-and-one-half hours. By sunset on the following day this unit had seized all of its assigned objectives, and control of this operation passed from the Eighth Army to the Sixth Army.[28]

## The Payoff in the Philippines

The Eighth Army's second amphibious landing on Luzon was conducted on 31 January 1945 at Nasugbu, forty-five miles south of Manila. The assault troops for this operation were the Eleventh Airborne Division, commanded by Major General Joseph Swing, and the 511th Parachute Regiment, commanded by Colonel Orin Haugen. MacArthur's officially stated reason for this landing was to conduct a "reconnaissance in force to test the enemy defenses in Southern Luzon." Eichelberger was directed to land only one regimental Combat Team (188th Glider Regiment) initially. However, he was given the discretion to land the 187th Glider Regiment and to push north toward Manila if no opposition was encountered. In addition Eichelberger had the authority to airdrop the 511th Parachute Regiment to exploit success if the situation warranted it. General MacArthur hoped that this operation would divert Japanese forces from north of Manila and prohibit them from concentrating their defenses against the Sixth Army.[29]

MacArthur's plan for this landing was daring and dangerous. He was sending one division to attack Manila from the south at a time when two full corps were getting nowhere from the north. The division MacArthur selected—the Eleventh Airborne—was the smallest division in the theater. It had only 8,321 soldiers, which was approximately half the size of a normal American division. It had one parachute infantry regiment of three battalions and two glider infantry regiments of two battalions each. This unit had almost no vehicles because airborne units were expected to be dropped by airplanes very near their target.

Whatever the Eleventh Airborne Division lacked in quantity, it more than made up for in quality. Eichelberger believed that this was the best division in the United States Army. All its enlisted men were highly motivated volunteers who were willing to jump out of an airplane or ride the dangerous and rickety glider to the battlefield. The officers in this division were also exceptional. Many were regular army officers and there was a large percentage of West Pointers at every echelon of command from platoon through division. This was a unit with a great deal of discipline and morale.

General Joseph Swing was the epitome of a division commander. He was a West Point classmate of Omar Bradley and Dwight Eisenhower. Bradley had hand-picked him to be the division artillery commander of the Eighty-second Division when he had that division. General Swing was the Hollywood image of a general, "tall, slender, prematurely white-haired, eagle-eyed and sharp featured." He had ruthlessly weeded out the weak, inept, and lazy and had honed his unit to a razor's edge. Swing believed in leadership by example and consistently located himself at his division's most dangerous position.[30]

Although Eichelberger was responsible for more than 200,000 soldiers, the Leyte mop up, and the planning of several important future operations, he decided to accompany the Eleventh Airborne Division on its risky assault on Manila. This decision was in direct violation of MacArthur's policy on army commanders taking personal control of troops once they had landed. MacArthur's brilliant plans officer, Major General Stephen Chamberlin, attempted to dissuade Eichelberger from this action on 27 January. Eichelberger used all his tact and diplomacy to convince Chamberlin of the necessity of this action. Eichelberger argued that he would not command the troops; Swing would. Eichelberger was initially to put only one regiment, the 188th Glider Infantry, ashore. If this unit received little opposition, he could send in the 187th Infantry Regiment to exploit the initial success of the 188th Infantry. Eichelberger told Chamberlin that only he was authorized by MacArthur to allow the 511th Parachute Regiment to jump in Luzon, and he could only make that decision from the front. After a lengthy discussion, Chamberlin supported Eichelberger's decision.[31]

In the eleven days from 31 January to 10 February 1945, Eichelberger's small force proved more successful than General MacArthur had hoped. Eichelberger, as an army commander, would enhance his reputation as the Fireman who would successfully handle the most impossible of assignments. The Nasugbu landing was the first opportunity for MacArthur to observe the new Eighth Army in action. Their performance would win his unstinted praise and admiration.

At 0815 hours on 31 January 1945, Eichelberger landed his first assault force (the 188th Regimental Combat Team) at Nasugbu Beach. This regiment encountered light resistance from the Japanese and rapidly drove inland. By 0945 this aggressive unit had seized the town of Nasugbu and the Nasugbu airport. At 1030 hours Eichelberger, aboard the U.S.S. *Spencer,* made the decision to exploit the initial success of the 188th Regimental Combat Team. He ordered General Swing to land the rest of the Eleventh Airborne Division and to push on as quickly as possible toward Manila. By noon the rest of the division had landed and was driving inland.[32]

Eichelberger went ashore at 1300 hours and immediately proceeded to the front to confer with General Swing. As usual, Eichelberger believed that a leader should go to the critical location on the battlefield to obtain firsthand the information needed to make decisions. Eichelberger, who was not without personal ambition, strongly desired to capture Manila quickly. He wanted to show MacArthur and Krueger who the best army commander in the theater was. In order to accomplish this ambitious goal, Eichelberger demanded speed throughout this operation. Once contact was made with the enemy, Eichelberger would not give them a chance to breathe until they had been either "dispersed or annihilated." Eichelberger's tactics, which demanded rapid penetration by his infantry in order to avoid the stalemate that would ensue if the Japanese had time to establish their defenses, had been developed at Buna and Biak, where he found the infantry had a tendency to go slow and wait for the artillery to defeat the enemy.[33]

Eichelberger's emphasis on speed was rewarded when lead elements of the 188th Regiment seized the important Palico River bridge, eight miles inland, at 1430 hours. The Japanese had prepared this bridge for demolition, but were surprised by the rapid advance of the Eleventh Airborne Division. The Japanese were caught on the far side of the bridge, and the intense fire from the Americans prevented them from reaching their demolitions. The Japanese retreated, leaving the bridge intact. This bridge was very important because it allowed Eichelberger's forces to use the Nasugbu-Tagaytay road, which was an all-weather highway, and considerably shortened their supply line. Failure to seize this bridge would have dramatically slowed the advance and possibly given the Japanese the opportunity to recover from their shock and confusion.[34]

After the bridge was seized, Eichelberger ordered General Swing to continue the advance through the night because he believed that the "enemy troops were confused and retreating, and a halt at dark would have permitted them to reorganize." At midnight the 187th Regiment passed through the 188th and continued the advance toward Manila. The Eleventh Airborne Division pushed on throughout the night. The following morning Eichelberger went to the front to inspect and exhort his men, and soon found himself moving with the lead company in the advance. His emphasis on speed had paid great dividends in his first twenty-eight hours ashore. The Eleventh Airborne Division, in this time, not only established a port and an airfield, but also penetrated the main line of Japanese resistance and advanced nineteen miles. To exploit this success Eichelberger alerted the 511th Parachute Regiment to be prepared for an airborne drop in the vicinity of Tagaytay Ridge. Although airborne operations were a relatively new concept, Eichelberger's creative intellect had incisively grasped their potential for disrupting the enemy's defenses. He was always looking for innovative tactics that would save American lives. The coherence of the Japanese defense would be destroyed when they found themselves fighting in two directions at once, after the paratroopers had landed behind them.[35]

By 2 February 1945 the Eleventh Airborne Division had fought its way through two Japanese defensive positions and by dusk had reached the third and most powerful Japanese position in the vicinity of Tagaytay Ridge, the most important military position held by the Japanese in southern Luzon. It was a formidable obstacle because, at 2,400 feet high, it dominated all the terrain in the region. Also, there was a two-lane concrete highway that led from Tagaytay Ridge straight down (thirty miles) into Manila. Therefore, as General Eichelberger and General Swing personally moved forward with the lead elements on 2 February, Eichelberger made the decision to envelop the Japanese positions on Tagaytay Ridge by airdropping the 511th Parachute Regiment behind the Japanese. The Japanese would then be in a crossfire between both United States elements.[36]

At 0730 hours on 3 February 1945, the 188th Regimental Combat Team, commanded by Colonel Robert Soule, assaulted the highest hill on Tagaytay Ridge, in order to fix the attention of the Japanese to their front. Forty-five minutes later the 511th Parachute Regiment jumped behind the Japanese positions on Tagaytay Ridge. The 511th was a superbly trained unit led by Colonel "Hardrock" Haugen. Haugen was an inspirational leader who was held in complete awe by his troops. He was a stern disciplinarian and a demanding taskmaster, yet he always led by example. At age thirty-eight, he could still outrun and outshoot any man in the regiment. His soldiers would follow him anywhere. Eichelberger was again under fire as he observed Haugen's and Soule's troops attack and destroy the Japanese position on Tagaytay Ridge. By 1300 hours Japanese resistance had been eliminated and these two units had linked up. As soon as Tagaytay Ridge was secure, patrols were sent down the highway to Manila. Meanwhile, Eichelberger, who had a great deal of compassion for his soldiers, went to a field hospital to cheer up his wounded men.[37]

General Swing was in complete agreement with Eichelberger's tactical philosophy. He realized that the Japanese had been surprised and psychologically unhinged by the Nasugbu landing and rapid advance. If he did not continue to push the advance, the Japanese would recover their equilibrium and re-form their defenses. During the night of 3–4 February, Swing ordered Colonel Haugen and one battalion to load onto trucks and proceed toward Manila until they encountered stiff resistance. The rest of the division, despite lack of sleep, followed on foot. This bold and imaginative decision by Swing proved to be exactly right. Haugen pushed forward so quickly that the Japanese were unable to blow up any bridges along the highway, although the demolitions had been placed. Consequently the advance was not slowed until they reached the town of Imus just south of Manila.[38]

At 1000 hours on 4 February 1945 Eichelberger had reached Imus and was moving with the forward-most elements of the 511th Parachute Regiment. The main highway bridge at Imus had been destroyed by the Japanese, and an alternate crossing bridge, 500 yards to the west, was heavily defended. However, the rugged paratroopers were too well trained to attempt a bloody frontal assault. They simply found a crossing site downstream and destroyed the Japanese positions from the rear. Eichelberger, who always gravitated to the most crucial location on the battlefield, almost lost his life in this operation. He was so close to the fighting that he was pinned down at the south end of this bridge by Japanese snipers.[39]

As soon as this crossing site had been secured, the paratroopers loaded onto their trucks and continued toward Manila. Eichelberger again positioned himself at the most dangerous part of the operation and traveled with this leading element until it reached Las Pinas, a southern suburb of Manila. The aggressiveness of this advance again paid off when the Las Pinas bridge was captured before the Japanese could set off their demolitions. The audacious paratroopers did not stop their advance until 2130 hours that evening, when they were halted by well-prepared Japanese positions at the Paranque bridge. By 4 February the Eleventh Airborne had traveled forty-five miles and had reached Manila.[40]

During this operation Eichelberger seemed to be everywhere at once. After the 511th Parachute Regiment crossed the Las Pinas bridge, Eichelberger found that the truck shuttling system was not functioning properly. He returned to Tagaytay to straighten out the problem. The next morning Eichelberger again displayed great personal courage and moved with the advance elements of the 511th Parachute Regiment across the Paranque bridge. However, this was the end of the rapid movement by the Eighth Army. The Americans had reached the Japanese Genko-Line which had been designed to protect Manila from an attack from the south. The Genko-Line was held by the Japanese Third Naval Battalion. This formidable obstacle was composed of camouflaged, reinforced concrete pillboxes, constructed on the southern edge of the city. These pillboxes, which were hard to locate, had large-caliber guns and a large quantity of anti-aircraft batteries. Against these positions, the Eleventh Airborne was able to move only 2,000 yards in two days.[41]

On 7 February 1945 Eichelberger received word from MacArthur that the Eleventh Airborne would soon come under Sixth Army control. Eichelberger departed Luzon before Manila was captured on 9 February 1945 in order to prepare for the southern Philippines campaign.

MacArthur had two reasons for ordering Eichelberger to conduct the Nasugbu landing, and Eichelberger successfully accomplished both of them. The official objective was to disrupt the Japanese lines of communication and to create a diversion that would siphon Japanese troops from the north side of Manila. However, MacArthur, who had studied human nature for his forty-two years of military service, had another motive—to stir Krueger to action. He realized that Krueger would be jealous of Eichelberger's success and would adopt a more audacious plan of advance to beat him into Manila. An eyewitness, Major General William C. Dunckel, wrote Eichelberger: "When you were pushing on Manila so rapidly, I visited Sixth Army Headquarters and found them greatly agitated over the fact that you would be in Manila before they were, and I believe to this day that we could have saved more of Manila if they had given you the means of coming in by way of Nasugbu." MacArthur's prodding of Krueger was very successful. By 4 February 1945 the Sixth

Army had two divisions, the First Cavalry and the Thirty-seventh Division, on the outskirts of Manila.[42]

The Luzon operation had been a complete triumph for Eichelberger. In 104 hours he had marched forty-five miles from Nasugbu to Bataan. He had goaded Krueger into action and he had once again solved a tactical dilemma for MacArthur. His reputation as the Fireman of the Southwest Pacific had been enhanced.

The key to the Eighth Army's success in this operation was the trilogy that Eichelberger had stressed since Buna—training, leadership, tactics. The highly disciplined, superbly conditioned paratroopers had moved day and night for 104 hours in order to accomplish their mission. They were mentally and physically prepared for the rigors of combat. Eichelberger kept the promise he had made to himself after Buna; his troops were better prepared than the Japanese. At all echelons of command, the Eleventh Airborne Division had displayed bold, imaginative, competent leadership. Commanders emulated Eichelberger and went to the critical location on the battlefield. The tactics were flexible and innovative. The Japanese were surprised and psychologically upset by the landing, and they were never able to recover. Once their initial defense was penetrated, they were unable to present a defense until they reached Manila. In this campaign it was the Japanese who knew fear as they vainly attempted to halt the onslaught of the American paratroopers.

After the Nasugbu operation, Eichelberger's relationship with MacArthur was significantly altered. Thereafter, MacArthur would always treat him with a great deal of warmth and kindness. He rewarded Eichelberger with a Silver Star, the nation's third highest award for gallantry in action, for his courage outside Manila, and he released a number of stories about the Eighth Army to the press. Eichelberger's performance had also had a profound impact on MacArthur's staff. The feisty air commander, General Kenney, told MacArthur that if "he wanted speed he should use" Eichelberger. He also found that the Bataan Gang was more friendly "than at any time since I have been in this theater." MacArthur did not surround himself (on his staff) with the most brilliant men in theater, but after Manila, even they were smart enough to realize that Eichelberger's performance had been extraordinary. They aped their chief's attitude toward Eichelberger.[43]

In sharp contrast to the mediocrity of MacArthur's staff is the performance of Eichelberger's staff during the Nasugbu operation. While Eichelberger was driving on Manila, his young and brilliant chief of staff, Clovis Byers, was working day and night to coordinate the Eighth Army's diverse responsibilities. Byers handled the Leyte mop up, supported the Nasugbu landing, and administered 200,000 troops throughout the theater. He also worked closely with his dynamic operations officer, Colonel Frank Bowen. Bowen, an infatiguable worker and tactical genius, drew up the plans for the Victor operations—the reconquest of the central and southern Philippines. The Victor operations required the Eighth Army to clear the Japanese from Palawan, Zamboanga, Panay, Negros, Cebu, Bohol, and Mindanao. However, in order for Eichelberger to accomplish this mission, MacArthur had to transfer five divisions, the Twenty-fourth, Thirty-first, Fortieth, Forty-first, and Americal, from the Sixth Army to the Eighth. This decision by MacArthur seriously curtailed the Sixth Army's operations on Luzon. Krueger felt that he needed every available division on Luzon to reduce Yamashita's formidable mountain strongholds. He deeply resented every man, weapon, or division that MacArthur took from him and gave to Eichelberger. After Manila, the competition between Eichelberger and Krueger was very fierce as they vied for MacArthur's accolades and assets. MacArthur, who may have had a blind spot in selecting his staff, brilliantly manipulated the talents and egos of these two superb army commanders.[44]

Eichelberger's execution of the Victor operations was flawless. As Krueger plodded forward against Yamashita on Luzon, the Eighth Army would conduct a clinic in amphibious warfare for the Japanese. In a series of lighting campaigns, Eichelberger opened the San Bernadino Strait and recaptured Palawan, Panay, Zamboanga, Bohol, the Sulu Archipelago, and twenty-two other of the Visayan Islands in the central and southern Philippines. Although the term "amphibious operations" has become synonymous with the Marine Corps, Eichelberger and the army conducted thirty-five amphibious assaults between 28 February and 3 April 1945. Eichelberger used his meager forces (he had five divisions to Krueger's fifteen) with great skill and daring. These amphibious landings ranged in size from company- to division-level task forces and all were successful. The coordination of these landings was complicated by the immense size of the Philippines, which measured 1,000 miles from north to

south. yet Eichelberger's efficient and imaginative staff never missed
a beat in the successful liberation of thirty islands in the central and
southern Philippines.[45]

Eichelberger demanded that his subordinates lead by example
and emphasize aggressive and innovative tactics. He had a healthy
respect for the tenacity and ability of the Japanese soldier. He did
not want any of his invasions to bog down into another Buna. He
realized the Japanese would never know where he would strike, and
he wanted his troops to capitalize on that surprise. Once the Japanese defense was breached, the Americans had to move fast before
the Japanese recovered. In order to ensure that his philosophy was
understood and implemented properly, Eichelberger inspected his
units personally. He got up early every morning and seldom went to
bed before midnight. During the day he made it his habit to fly to
the most crucial sector of his zone of action to advise and support his
subordinates. At the conclusion of the Victor operations, he could
boast of having been present during the liberation of every major
city on the thirty liberated islands.[46]

The Victor operations were Eichelberger's responsibility from
their inception. In this mission he would not be expected to correct
someone else's mistakes. It was a unique opportunity for him to
display his talents in the planning and execution of his own campaign, and he made the most of it.

His first campaigns were in the southwest Philippines—Palawan,
the Sulu Archipelago, and Zamboanga, which surround the Sulu
Sea. MacArthur wanted Eichelberger to eliminate Japanese resistance and to secure naval and air bases on these islands. The United
States Navy and Air Force were to cut the flow of Japanese supplies
from their homeland to the Dutch East Indies, making use of these
bases. To accomplish this demanding assignment, Eichelberger selected the Forty-first Division, whose training in small-unit tactics
he had personally supervised. Brigadier General Harold W. Haney
and the 186th Regimental Combat Team were responsible for capturing Palawan, while Major General Jens Doe and the remainder of
the division secured Zamboanga and Sulu.[47]

Eichelberger never left anything to chance. In order to ensure
that the officers and men in the 186th Regimental Combat Team
understood their orders and his expectations, he personally briefed
them a week before the invasion. On the day before the Palawan
invasion, he briefed the senior officers on the manner in which they

would conduct this campaign. He told them to advance boldly once they had landed rather than digging in and hoping that naval gunfire would defeat the Japanese. He believed that if his troops were aggressive, another Buna could be avoided. He was not disappointed by their performance. On 28 February 1945 at 0845 hours, the 186th Regimental Combat Team landed unopposed at Palawan. As Eichelberger flew over the landing site to observe the operation, he was pleased to see the 186th Infantry aggressively moving inland. At the end of the first day this unit had seized the important town of Puerto Princesa and the island's important airfields.[48]

The Japanese forces on Palawan were completely surprised by the American landing. As soon as they sighted the Americans, they withdrew into positions they had prepared in the densely wooded mountains in the interior of the island. This withdrawal served no strategic purpose, since they abandoned the population centers and the airfields to the Americans. However, the 186th Infantry did not rest on its laurels. They instituted a vigorous patrolling to locate and destroy the enemy. In the first week of March this unit proved the success of Eichelberger's training program as it pursued, isolated, and destroyed all organized Japanese resistance on the island. By 20 March the Eighth Army Engineers had an all-weather airstrip operational on the island, and the campaign was completed by the end of March.[49]

On 9 March 1945 Eichelberger celebrated his fifty-ninth birthday. The following day, at 0915 hours, General Jens Doe and the Forty-first Division (less the 186th Regiment) landed on the Zamboanga Peninsula. The Japanese offered little resistance at the beaches, and Eichelberger personally came ashore at noon to ensure that the momentum of the attack was maintained. General Doe, who had performed so well on Biak, pushed his troops hard and captured Zamboanga City the next day. The Japanese, as they had at Palawan, withdrew into prepared defenses in the mountains. However, the Japanese were not prepared for the determined assault by the Forty-first Division on their positions. On 24 March Doe broke through the defensive stronghold of the Japanese, ending organized resistance in the region. As one regiment spearheaded this mission, Doe sent his other regiment on a series of electrifying amphibious landings to secure the Bongao Islands, Sanga Sanga, and Jolo Island. All of these operations were overwhelming successes and a credit to Eichelberger's emphasis on small-unit training and initiative at all levels. This campaign resulted in the liberation of more than 250,000 Filipinos in addition to capturing important airfields that could be used to interdict Japanese naval convoys.[50]

At the same time that the Forty-first Division was performing so admirably on Palawan and Zamboanga, Eichelberger commenced the liberation of the southern Visayans (Panay, Negros, Cebu, and Bohol). The Fortieth Division, commanded by Major General Rapp Brush, was responsible for Panay and Negros Occidental; the Americal Division, commanded by Major General William H. Arnold, for Cebu, Bohol, and Negros Oriental. Despite the myriad of complex details to be coordinated in these diverse operations, Eichelberger's dynamic staff never failed him. They juggled the limited logistical and transportation assets between operations with great skill and daring. Their imagination, flexibility, and adaptability enabled Eichelberger to visit the front with complete confidence that the administrative problems would be solved.

Eichelberger had received the Fortieth Division from General Krueger because the latter lacked confidence in its ability. Krueger felt the division had not performed well on Luzon in January. However, Eichelberger had a great deal of confidence in General Brush. In early March he briefed Brush on his tactical philosophy of rapid penetration and vigorous pursuit. He further briefed him on the horror of Buna and what could occur if he (Brush) were timid in his advance. At 0905 hours on 18 March, the Fortieth Division (less the 108th Regimental Combat Team) landed on Panay. The Fortieth Division, known also as the Rattlesnake Division, in its first twenty-four hours ashore lived up to this name. They rapidly drove inland and captured the capital city, Iloilo. The Japanese defenders of Panay offered only sporadic resistance before they fled in disorder to the mountains. Eichelberger was very proud of the performance of the Fortieth Division. They had fulfilled the dream he had had since Buna of watching the Japanese flee in fear from American veterans.[51]

On 23 March Eichelberger was summoned to Manila for a conference with General MacArthur. MacArthur spoke to Eichelberger for over two hours. He had pitted his two army commanders against each and had played on their egos and natural competitiveness. However, Krueger had recently been promoted to four-star general, and MacArthur tried to soften this blow for Eichelberger. He showered his Eighth Army commander with praise for his successful operations on Palawan, Zamboanga, Panay, and the Sulu Archipelago. He then expressed his disappointment at the ponderous advance of the Sixth Army on Luzon. Although MacArthur did not really explain why Eichelberger wasn't promoted, he did boost his morale. In reality MacArthur had never realized how good an army commander Eichelberger would be until the recent campaigns. Krueger was the most senior army commander in the theater. On seniority alone he deserved the promotion and, in honesty, he had never been defeated.[52]

On 24 March, when Eichelberger had become convinced that the Japanese resistance on Panay had collapsed, he established a landing date for the Negros invasion—29 March. Eichelberger hoped to strike the Japanese garrison of 13,500 men on Negros before they had an opportunity to build up their defenses, thus exploiting the success of the Panay operation.

Today, the general opinion of the American army is that it lumbered slowly to victory, massing its overwhelming superiority of men and materiel against an impoverished foe. A close look at the Negros operation will show that this stereotype is untrue—and unfair to the soldiers who served in the Philippines.

At 0505 hours on 29 March 1945, four-and-one-half hours before the division landed, Lieutenant Aaron A. Hanson and a reinforced platoon from Company F, 185th Infantry, landed on Negros. The mission of this raiding party was to seize the 650-foot steel truss Bago River bridge before the Fortieth Division landed. Since the bridge had been mined and prepared for demolition, the only way to take this objective was to rush across its full span and then kill the Japanese on the far side before they could blow up the bridge. In a sharp thirty-minute fire-fight that commenced at 0730 hours, Lieutenant Hanson seized the bridge and killed the guards before they could detonate the demolitions. Hanson then held the bridge until relieved by the remainder of the division. The speed, audacity, and violence of execution by this young lieutenant was the key to success in this entire operation. If this bridge, across a deep chasm, had not been seized, the whole operation might not have been successful.

There were eight other bridges, all prepared for demolition, along the route from the landing site to the island's capital, Bacolod. If Hanson had not captured this first bridge, then the Japanese would certainly have had enough time to blow the others. However, the American advance was so rapid after they crossed the Bago River bridge that all the Japanese were seized before the charges could be detonated. On 30 March the city of Bacolod was taken with very little destruction. Eichelberger believed that "lives can be saved by speed." If his troops had not advanced so quickly, Eichelberger believed that the capital would have been destroyed and the Fortieth Division's casualties much higher.[53]

In the first week of April, the Japanese used small delaying forces to slow the advance of the Fortieth Division as they hastily tried to prepare defenses in the rugged interior of the island. However, the Rattlesnake Division struck fast and hard into the Japanese main line of defense and drove them from their positions. The highly motivated, superbly led Fortieth Division killed 7,525 Japanese in six weeks at a cost of 381 American dead.[54]

MacArthur was so impressed by the speed with which this campaign was concluded that he told Clovis Byers to "Tell Bob that landing of Brush's to secure that long concrete bridge was brilliant strategy. Bob's whole operation is good."[55]

On 26 March 1945, between the Panay and Negros operations, Eichelberger landed the Americal Division (less the 164th Regiment) on the island of Cebu. As had become the pattern in these operations, the Japanese offered no resistance on the coastal plain and withdrew into the interior. However, this unit was unable to make a rapid drive on the populous capital of the island, Cebu City, because the Japanese had prepared extensive minefields on the beaches. These minefields and other obstacles inflicted heavy casualties on the Americal Division. The Americans were able to breach these obstacles only with great difficulty and did not reach Cebu City, the second largest port in the Philippines, until the following day. Unfortunately, this short delay was enough for the Japanese to destroy the city before they retreated into the mountainous interior.

The Japanese mountain strongholds on Cebu were far more formidable than those encountered on the other islands. They had spent months preparing honeycombed positions in the steep hills above the harbor. Many of the tunnels and pillboxes were constructed of concrete and steel. These heavily fortified positions prevented the Americal Division from advancing for more than a week. General Arnold, who at forty-four was one of the youngest division commanders in the American army, had a plan. He was a veteran of some very tough fighting on Bougainville in the Solomons, and he was loathe to conduct a frontal assault against these positions. He requested that Eichelberger release the 164th Regiment back to him. This Eichelberger did on 9 April 1945. Arnold used innovative tactics to surprise the enemy, reduce the effectiveness of his weapons, and unnerve the Japanese soldiers. He ordered the 164th Regiment, guided by guerrillas, to move twenty-five miles by night marches to take up positions behind the Japanese. then in a move that resembled the Tagaytay Ridge operation, the Americal Division conducted a coordinated attack against the Japanese from two directions and shattered their defenses. On 20 April organized Japanese resistance on Cebu was declared officially over. The Americal Division then conducted amphibious landings on Bohol and Negros Oriental on 11 and 26 April 1945. Both operations were overwhelming successes.[56]

Eichelberger's success in the central and southern Philippines enhanced MacArthur's reputation as a military genius. While the bulk of his forces were tied up in the methodical advance of the Sixth Army on Luzon, Eichelberger's bold and audacious campaigns occupied the headlines for MacArthur. Good publicity always brought out the best in MacArthur, and he cabled Eichelberger:

> Please accept for yourself and extend to General Brush,
> General Doe, General Arnold, and all officers and men
> involved my heartiest commendation for their brilliant
> execution of the Visayan campaign. This [is a] model of what
> a light but aggressive command can accomplish in rapid
> exploitation.[57]

MacArthur told General Byers "that Bob's progress in these Eighth Army operations was brilliant and that nothing in the history of this war would surpass what Bob [had] done with the meager forces available to him in such lightning-like strokes." On 10 April 1945 Eichelberger was summoned to a meeting with MacArthur, who stated that the operations in Palawan, Zamboanga, the Sulu Archipelago, and the Visayans had been executed "just the way he would have wanted to have done it had he been an Army commander—speed, dash, brilliance, etc." MacArthur's operations officer told Eichelberger that the "Visayan campaign would some day be considered a classic."[58]

Eichelberger, who was a very sensitive and ambitious officer, relished this high praise from General MacArthur. More than just doing a good job, Eichelberger always sought the approval of

MacArthur. He was bitterly disappointed at his treatment after Buna, but after the Visayan campaign he was MacArthur's favorite commander. His reputation shone even brighter when compared to Krueger's plodding on Luzon. MacArthur described Krueger as an "old fashioned general who wants to do everything by the rules." MacArthur confided to Eichelberger that every time he assigned a mission to the Sixth Army they always protested that they needed twice the numbers of troops allocated. However, Eichelberger's Eighth Army was always innovative enough to win victories with the number of troops allocated for the operations.[59]

By 20 April 1945 Eichelberger had liberated 6.5 million Filipinos and 33,000 square miles of Philippine territory. The only Japanese resistance left in the entire archipelago was centered in northern Luzon and in Mindanao. MacArthur wanted Mindanao liberated quickly and the 50,000 Japanese troops on that island destroyed. In order to accomplish this demanding assignment, he sent in his best—Eichelberger. This was to be Eichelberger's finest hour and most brilliant campaign. At Mindanao, Eichelberger paid the Japanese back for the educational experience at Buna. It was a complete vindication of his rugged training program, as well as emphasis on leadership by example and utilization of flexible and innovative tactics. In this campaign he defeated and humiliated an enemy possessing superior combat strength.[60]

Despite his inability to release a large number of troops for the operation, General MacArthur strongly desired that the 95,000 Filipinos on Mindanao be liberated from the Japanese occupation. He fully realized that Mindanao was a difficult undertaking for two reasons. For one thing, the size of the island, which was 36,546 square miles, the second largest in the archipelago, made it difficult for an attacking force to secure. Even more important, however, was the strength and disposition of the enemy garrison on Mindanao. The Japanese had originally expected MacArthur to commence his invasion of the Philippines with Mindanao. Therefore the 50,000 Japanese on the island had been preparing their defenses for three years.

The bulk of these forces was concentrated in Davao, which was the island's largest and most important city. The Japanese fully expected the Americans to conduct a frontal attack on the island through Davao Gulf. Therefore they had built up strong coastal de-

*Forged by Fire*

fenses along the shoreline, which included a large concentration of artillery and anti-aircraft batteries. Furthermore, the entire gulf was heavily mined to prevent an amphibious landing. The Japanese had also prepared their defenses in depth, in order to protract the campaign as long as possible. They anticipated withdrawing into the jungle by falling back from Davao into prepared defensive bunkers.[61]

General MacArthur was well aware of the strength of the Japanese fortifications on Mindanao through his Intelligence system. The fighting on Luzon had also prepared him for the tenacity with which the Japanese would fight to hold onto the island. In April 1945 the campaign on Luzon had already lasted for three months, and by war's end it would still not be over. However, MacArthur was confident that Davao City could be captured in four months and the huge harbor in Davao Gulf opened soon after.

To capture Davao City and to liberate the Filipino population of Mindanao, MacArthur could spare Eichelberger only a limited number of troops: the X Corps, commanded by Major General Franklin Sibert, the son of Eichelberger's first regimental commander in the Tenth Infantry Regiment; and two reinforced divisions— the Twenty-fourth and the Thirty-first. The Twenty-fourth Division was one of the best-trained units in the theater. Eichelberger had personally supervised its small-unit training in scouting, patrolling, and night operations before Hollandia. However, General Irving was no longer the division commander. On Leyte the division had encountered formidable opposition from the Japanese that MacArthur's Intelligence officer did not know existed. Subsequently their advance was slow, and Irving was relieved by Krueger. The next division did not do any better, and Irving was later vindicated. However, Eichelberger had to intervene personally to ensure that Irving was not railroaded. This division's new commander was Major General Roscoe Woodruff. Woodruff was a classmate of Eisenhower and Bradley at West Point and had been the first captain of the class. Tall and husky, Woodruff had a reputation for efficiency. He had been transferred from the European Theater shortly before D-Day because he did not have combat experience, which was a prerequisite for command in that operation. As a result Woodruff was anxious to do well in this operation in order to prove himself to those commanders in Europe who had transferred him. The Thirty-first Division was commanded by Major General Clarence Martin, who had served under Eichelberger at Buna and had subsequently thoroughly trained his troops in small-unit tactics.[62]

Eichelberger devised a brilliant plan for overcoming the superb defenses and numerical superiority of the Japanese on Mindanao. Instead of a frontal assault into the heavily mined Davao Gulf as the Japanese expected, he would land his troops at Illana Bay and then have the infantry march 100 miles through the jungle to take Davao City from the rear. He believed that if his troops moved quickly enough, the city could be seized before the Japanese had time to react. Success would depend on the speed and beachhead performance of the first units to land at the Illana Gulf.

At 0800 hours on 17 April 1945, the lead elements of the Twenty-fourth Division landed at Illana Bay on Mindanao. Eichelberger was present at the Twenty-fourth Division's landings and personally went ashore at 1000 hours to inspect the beachhead. He was not disappointed by the performance of the Twenty-fourth Division. The superior training in this division paid off in handsome dividends in the first twenty-four hours. Patrols from the Nineteenth and Twenty-first Infantry regiments displayed a great deal of aggressiveness in seeking out the enemy. These patrols moved quickly through the jungle, crossing chest-deep steams, and seized the first five days' objectives in less than twenty-four hours. In a tough night action, one patrol on the southern-most flank defeated a determined Japanese attack. By dawn the following day, the division had secured a thirty-five-mile strip on the coast and the important Malabang airstrip.[63]

At dawn on 18 April 1945, the Nineteenth Infantry Regiment commenced to move overland toward Davao Gulf along highway number 1. At the same time General Woodruff loaded the Twenty-first Infantry Regiment onto small riverboats and sent them on an audacious amphibious thrust up the Mindanao River. Since the Japanese had offered only light resistance, other than the one night attack, Eichelberger was determined to exploit success by pushing the Twenty-fourth Division toward Davao Gulf with as much speed as possible. The advance of the Twenty-first Infantry up the Mindanao River was remarkable. To exploit the advantage of surprise and to prevent the Japanese from forming a defensive line, the river force moved both night and day. All Japanese resistance along the river was quickly destroyed by the aggressive small-unit patrolling of the

Twenty-first Infantry. The realistic training of the Twenty-fourth Division before the operation was rewarded in several successful night attacks on the river, which resulted in the complete demoralization of the Japanese in the region. This force moved forty-three miles inland in just thirty-one hours. The rapid advance of these two regiments kept the enemy off balance and prevented them from establishing a line of defense. Both forces linked up at Fort Pikit, fifty-two miles inland, on 22 April 1945, and then prepared to march overland to attack the town of Digos on the coast of Davao Gulf.[64]

On the same day the Thirty-first Division landed at Illana Bay and commenced its advance behind the Twenty-fourth Division. On 28 April the Twenty-fourth Division seized the town of Digos and turned northward to march on Davao City. In just twelve days the division had marched 110 miles through a difficult jungle to cross the island of Mindanao and seized a foothold on Davao Gulf. MacArthur was ecstatic when he heard that Digos had been taken. He paid Eichelberger one of his greatest compliments when he said, "You run an army in combat just like I would like to have done it."[65]

On 30 April 1945 the Twenty-fourth Division commenced its drive up the coastal plain from Digos to Davao City. The Twenty-fourth Division history recorded the importance of attacking Davao from the rear: "The 'wrong way' invasion had encountered excellent emplacements lining the road—useless because most firelanes pointed east. In effect, the division's offensive proceeded along a route which the Japs had earmarked for a fighting retreat. The enemy was caught off balance and he was kept that way." Three days later, on 3 May 1945, the Twenty-fourth Division seized Davao City.[66] Although the campaign dragged on for six more weeks as the X Corps pursued the remnants of the Japanese army into the jungle, the strategic victory on Mindanao was secured with the capture of Davao City.

Eichelberger was able to accomplish his mission in two weeks because he had successfully identified Davao City as the enemy's operational center of gravity. He realized that the Japanese were only prepared to defend Davao City from a frontal attack. They had not prepared any significant defenses for an attack from the landward direction. Once ashore, speed and aggressiveness were the hallmark of this operation. The Twenty-fourth Division moved so fast that the surprised Japanese were continually off balance and were never able to constitute a formidable defense. Once Davao City fell, the entire defense of the island was unhinged and the effectiveness of the Japanese army rapidly deteriorated.

The Mindanao campaign was the high point of Eichelberger's career as an army commander. It also cemented a change in MacArthur's attitude toward him. Initially the Eighth Army had a supporting role in the theater and Krueger was MacArthur's favorite commander. However, Eichelberger's performance had dramatically altered this perception. After Eichelberger's audacious drive on Manila in February with the Eleventh Airborne Division, MacArthur and his staff "applauded" and developed a more "friendly" attitude toward the Eighth Army. His execution of the Zamboanga-Sulu Archipelago operation resulted in loud praise. The rapid conclusion of the Visayan campaign put Eichelberger and Eighth Army in "high favor" with MacArthur. However, Eichelberger's capture of Davao City in twelve days, when MacArthur expected the campaign to last at least four months, marked the Eighth Army as the best in the theater. MacArthur's staff described the Mindanao campaign as "one of the most brilliant in American Annals."[67]

In fact, MacArthur was so impressed with Eichelberger's conduct of this difficult assignment that on 3 June 1945 he asked Eichelberger to be his chief of staff. Sutherland had got himself involved with a young Australian woman and MacArthur decided to relieve him. This incident also gave MacArthur the opportunity to revamp his staff. Eichelberger, who could be ruthless with incompetents, would have dramatically improved the efficiency and attitude of several members of the Bataan Gang. They would have performed their jobs properly or Eichelberger would have relieved them. However, flattered by the offer, though Eichelberger was, he had waited too long to command an army to give it up for this position. He politely refused.[68]

On 1 July 1945 MacArthur assigned Eichelberger and the Eighth Army one last mission—to mop up the Japanese on Luzon. Japanese resistance on northern Luzon was still not broken. The Sixth Army claimed that only 23,000 Japanese were left in the mountains, but this was another gross underestimation. In reality, Yamashita had 65,000 soldiers skillfully emplaced in the mountains and was far from beaten. He was still conducting a brilliant defense. However, Eichelberger had barely begun the methodical destruction of these mountain strongholds when the atomic bombs were dropped on Nagasaki and Hiroshima, which ended the war.[69]

Eichelberger commanded the Eighth Army in combat for almost a year. In that short period of time he put his stamp on this army. He molded it into the finest fighting force in any nation during World War II. This army did not rely on overwhelming resources to win; rather, it used audacious and innovative tactics to cut through the Japanese defenses with the skill of a surgeon. He was successful because he applied the lessons he had learned at Buna. In that brutal battle, the Japanese had held all the high cards. However, in the course of putting out that fire for MacArthur, Eichelberger was permanently changed. He promised himself that he would never again enter combat with troops that were unprepared for battle. As an army commander he kept that promise. His troops were physically tough and mentally prepared for every situation they would encounter. He demanded that leaders at all echelons of command set the example for their soldiers. He wanted officers to show initiative, be willing to take risks, and locate themselves at the most dangerous point of action. He himself set the tone in the theater by leading his soldiers into Manila, Cebu City, and Davao City.

Eichelberger was an inspirational leader with a uniquely personal touch. The Eighth Army conducted fifty-five amphibious assaults—each one successful. Yet, while orchestrating these many diverse operations, Eichelberger never let himself forget the needs and aspirations of the young men who made up his army. He made a point of talking to them before they went into battle and was present with them during the fighting. After an operation he visited the mess halls to ensure they were fed properly, and the hospitals to console the wounded. He also conducted numerous award ceremonies to reward his soldiers for their courage under fire.

Eichelberger's reputation as an army commander was known and admired even in the European Theater. His classmate General George Patton wrote him, "In my limited experience with amphibious attacks, I found them the most dangerous form of sport yet devised. If I should be so fortunate, I am going to sit at your feet and learn how to do it." However, the highest accolade came from MacArthur, who succinctly summed up Eichelberger's performance as an army commander when he stated: "No Army of the war has achieved greater glory and distinction than the Eighth."[70]

# Epilogue: The Sunset Years

ON 30 AUGUST 1945 EICHELBERGER STEPPED FROM THE CRAMPED CON-
fines of a transport plane onto Japanese soil. He had arrived at the
airfield at Atsugi, twenty miles southwest of Tokyo, to coordinate
the security of General MacArthur, who was due to arrive shortly.
Eichelberger was worried because he did not trust the Japanese,
who had four million soldiers on their home islands while he had
only the Eleventh Airborne Division. However, his fears proved un-
founded. MacArthur landed without incident and proceeded from
the airfield to his new headquarters at Yokohama, unmolested. As
the automobile slowly proceeded toward MacArthur's headquarters,
Eichelberger reflected on the difference between the day's bloodless
events and his long-anticipated invasion of Japan. MacArthur, before the Japanese surrender, had anticipated landing Eichelberger's
Eighth Army with three corps and ten divisions on the Tokyo plain.
This assault was intended to be the knockout blow that would capture the heartland of Japan and end the war. Eichelberger had
feared it would be a very bloody campaign and was elated to have
been spared its execution.

During this trip Eichelberger was informed of the future missions
of the Eighth Army in Japan. He was to occupy key strategic cities
throughout Japan and to facilitate the demobilization of the four
million Japanese still in uniform. He was to liberate all Allied prisoners and arrest suspected war criminals. He was also to assist in the
release of all political prisoners in Japan. In all these complex assignments, over the next few months, the efficiency, discipline, and re-
straint of the Eighth Army were exemplary. The performance of the
Eighth Army was as admirable in peacetime as it had been in war.[1]

In November 1945 General Dwight D. Eisenhower replaced Marshall as the chief of staff of the United States Army. Eisenhower
wanted Eichelberger to be his deputy chief of staff in Washington,

because he liked and trusted him. He also wanted a senior officer from the Pacific Theater to balance his own European experience. Together they would have ensured that officers from both theaters were treated equally as the army adjusted to its peacetime missions. MacArthur did not openly oppose Eichelberger's transfer to Washington. Instead, he used a more devious method to convince Eichelberger to stay in Japan. He told Eichelberger that if he went to Washington, Krueger would be given command of the Eighth Army in the occupation of Japan. Eichelberger was afraid that, if he left, the careers of the most faithful staff officers and commanders would be ruined by Krueger. He believed that Krueger would destroy his subordinates' future because of the dislike and competitiveness he felt for Eichelberger. (In fairness to Krueger, it should be noted that there is no indication anywhere in his papers that he possessed any vindictive intentions.) As MacArthur had hoped, Eichelberger turned down Eisenhower's request and remained in Japan.[2]

Eichelberger remained in Japan for three more years as the commander of the Eighth Army. In this position he supervised ports and railways, commanded the military government units, and oversaw the construction of modern airfields and roads throughout Japan. He also acted as a mentor to the officers who had served under him during the war. He was very conscientious in assisting them in getting promoted or selected to the schools or assignments they desired. He never lost his feel for the individual despite the fact that the army had become a large bureaucracy. He tried to further the careers of all his subordinates. His success in evidenced by two examples— Clovis Byers and Frank Bowen. Both these young officers finished their careers as lieutenant generals.

After three years of occupation duty, Eichelberger decided to retire. His wife had inherited money, so he had no financial worries. His purpose in retiring was to write about his experiences in the Pacific. He believed that the Eighth Army had never been properly recognized for its accomplishments in the war, and he very much hoped to rectify that oversight. On 31 December 1948 Eichelberger retired from the army. He was sixty-four years old and in the best of physical health. In September 1949 the *Saturday Evening Post* published a series of seven articles by Eichelberger entitled "Our Jungle Road to Tokyo," in which he wrote about the Eighth Army's combat record. The following year these articles were used as the basis for a book of the same title. Although Eichelberger stressed the contributions of the Eighth Army to the war effort, he made no mention of the personality clashes in the Pacific Theater. His book was very complimentary toward MacArthur and did not hint of any controversy.[3]

As Eichelberger was finishing his literary projects, the Korean War broke out. The then under secretary of the army, Tracy S. Voorhees, requested that Eichelberger come to Washington to work for him as a special adviser on the Far East. What Voorhees really needed was a special adviser on the personality of Douglas MacArthur. Eichelberger accepted this job and assisted in Washington for over a year. However, in the spring of 1951, his wife felt it was time for him to retire completely. They owned a beautiful home in Asheville, North Carolina, her hometown, and she wanted to settle there permanently. So, at the age of sixty-seven, Eichelberger retired a second time.

Eichelberger and his wife spent their last years together in Asheville. Yet Eichelberger never really retired. He was too dynamic a personality to sit at home and do nothing. He wrote numerous articles and lectures on varied political and military topics. He also became an avid golfer in order to keep himself physically fit.

As time passed, Eichelberger began to reflect more and more on the Pacific War. He also became increasingly annoyed by his perception of how MacArthur had treated him. He had started the war senior to Eisenhower, Bradley, and Patton. Yet he had never been promoted to four-star general and, despite his book, his campaigns were virtually unknown to the American public. However, the exploits of Eisenhower and his classmate Patton were very well known. He felt that he had not been properly appreciated by MacArthur and was increasingly incensed by the heroic articles that continued to appear about his old boss in newspapers and magazines. Although personally bitter, Eichelberger never publicly impugned the honor or integrity of MacArthur. However, he did indirectly inform MacArthur of his resentment. Every year on MacArthur's birthday, all his closest staff officers and commanders gathered for a celebration in New York City. Eichelberger always declined to attend. Every year his absence was noted, and MacArthur would ask Clovis Byers about Eichelberger and praise his military prowess.[4]

Often in the years before his death on 27 September 1961, Eichelberger's active mind returned to the Pacific battlefields of World War II—the scene of his greatest accomplishments, when he had to lead men in desperate battle against a formidable opponent, to the time when he built a legendary reputation as the Fireman of the Southwest Pacific.

The key to Eichelberger's success was his ability to adapt to the experiences he had encountered at Buna. Although he was fifty-six years old at the time of this battle, he had not grown inflexible and staid in his thinking. He possessed a creative intellect and was always willing to try new ideas. He developed a tough and realistic training program, which mentally and physically conditioned his soldiers for combat. He weeded out incompetent leaders and promoted those young men who were willing to place themselves in harm's way and lead by example. He also demanded that his leaders use innovative and flexible tactics to defeat the enemy. He would not allow methodical, dull-witted frontal attacks, which results in high casualties. Instead, he outfoxed his opponents with speed and surprise.

At the time of his death in 1961, Eichelberger's accomplishments were little known in any part of the army. However, in the wake of the Vietnam War, as the American army sought to reform itself, it increasingly turned to the study of military history. In 1986 the army published a leadership manual for its senior officers, which studied the challenges and responsibilities of American commanders in battle, with the intention of educating today's senior army officers about the successful methods used to motivate American soldiers to overcome formidable obstacles to accomplish their mission. MacArthur was not selected as a case study in this important text, but Eichelberger was. He would have been pleased that twenty-five years after his death he was still serving as a mentor to the American army.

# ABBREVIATIONS

Alger, *DDMA:* John Alger, *Definitions and Doctrine of the Military Art.* (Wayne, N.J.: Avery Publishing Group, 1985).

Anders, *Gentle Knight:* Leslie Anders, *Gentle Knight: The Life and Times of Major General Edwin Forrest Harding.* (Kent, Ohio: Kent State Press, 1985).

Bradley, *General's Life:* Omar Bradley and Clay Blair, *A General's Life:* (New York: Simon and Schuster, 1983).

Craven and Cate, *Air Force:* Wesley Craven and James Cate (eds.) *The Army Air Forces in World War II* (Volume V): *The Pacific: Matterhorn to Nagasaki, June 1944 to August 1945.* (Chicago: University of Chicago Press, 1953).

Cullum, *Register of Graduates: Register of Graduates and Former Cadets of the United States Military Academy.* (West Point, N.Y.: Association of Graduates, USMA, 1983).

Eichelberger and MacKaye. *Jungle Road:* Robert Eichelberger and Milton MacKaye. *Our Jungle Road to Tokyo.* (New York: Viking Press, 1949).

English, *Infantry:* John English. *On Infantry.* (New York: Praeger Press, 1981).

FM 22–100: Field Manual 22–100 "Military Leadership" (Washington, D.C.: Department of the Army, 1983).

James, *Years of MacArthur:* D. Clayton James. *The Years of MacArthur:* (Volume II) *1941–1945.* (Boston: Houghton-Mifflin, Co., 1975).

Kenney, *General Kenney Reports:* George Kenney. *General Kenney Reports: A Personal History of the Pacific War.* (New York: Duell, Sloane and Pearle, 1949).

Krueger, *Down Under:* Walter Krueger. *From Down Under to Nippon: The Story of the Sixth Army in World War II.* (Washington, D.C.: Combat Forces Press, 1953).

Luvaas, "A Leavenworth Nightmare": Jay Luvaas, "Buna—A Leavenworth Nightmare," in *America's First Battles, 1776–1965.* Ed. Charles Heller and William Stofft (Lawrence, Kans.: University of Kansas Press, 1986).

Luvaas, *Miss Em:* Jay Luvaas. *Dear Miss Em: General Eichelberger's War in the Pacific, 1942–1945.* (Westport, Conn.: Greenwood Press, 1972).

MacArthur, *Reminiscences:* Douglas MacArthur. *Reminiscences.* (New York: McGraw-Hill, 1964).

# Forged by Fire

Mayo, *Bloody Buna:* Lida Mayo. *Bloody Buna.* (Garden City, N.Y.: Doubleday and Company, 1974).

Milner, *Victory:* Samuel Milner. *Victory in Papua.* (Washington, D.C.: Office of the Chief of Military History, 1957).

Nye, *Challenge of Command:* Roger Nye. *The Challenge of Command.* (Wayne, N.J.: Avery Publishing Group, 1986).

*Operations-FM100-5:* Field Manual 100-5 "Operations". (Washington, D.C.: Department of the Army, 1986).

*Papuan Campaign:* War Department, Military Intelligence Division, *Papuan Campaign: The Buna-Sanananda Operation 16 November 1942-23 January 1943*, American Forces in Action Series. (Washington, D.C.: War Department, 1944).

Riegelman, *Caves of Biak:* Harold Riegelman. *The Caves of Biak: An American Officer's Experience in the Southwest Pacific.* (New York: The Dial Press, 1955).

Smith, *Approach:* Robert Ross Smith. *The Approach to the Philippines.* (Washington, D.C.: Office of the Chief of Military History, 1953).

Smith, *Triumph:* Robert Ross Smith. *Triumph in the Philippines.* (Washington, D.C.: Office of the Chief of Military History, 1963).

Spector, *Eagle Against the Sun:* Ronald Spector. *Eagle Against the Sun.* New York: The Free Press, 1985).

Weigley. *Eisenhower's Lieutenants:* Russell Weigley. *Eisenhower's Lieutenants, The Campaigns of France and Germany, 1944-1945.* (Bloomington: Indiana University Press, 1981).

# NOTES

*Notes to Chapter 1*

1. All information relating to the early career of General Eichelberger is taken from his dictations, 1952–60, a complete copy of which is deposited in the William R. Perkins Library, Duke University, Durham, N.C. Hereafter cited as "Eichelberger Dictations."

2. Eichelberger Dictations (undated) to Virginia C. Westall.

3. Ibid.

4. Ibid.

5. George Eichelberger to Superintendent dated 18 October 1905 (located in the West Point Archives), West Point, N.Y.

6. Luvaas, *Miss Em*, p. 4; Martin Blumenson, *The Patton Papers* (Boston: Houghton-Mifflin, 1972), pp. 151, 174.

7. Eichelberger Dictations, 12 September 1958.

8. Eichelberger Dictations, 25 March 1955.

9. Eichelberger Dictations, 14 October 1957; USMA Special Collections. A brief note on decorations in necessary. The medal for the Silver Star was not instituted until 1932. Before that date a miniature silver star was worn on the ribbon of the Service Medal for the war in which the citation was won. This applies to all mentions of this award before World War II. For more information, see *The Medal of Honor of the United States Army* (Washington: Government Printing Office, 1948), p. 460.

10. Ibid.

11. Ibid.; and Eichelberger Dictations, 12 September 1958.

12. Eichelberger Dictations, 12 September 1958.

13. Eichelberger Dictation of 1954 contained in the Eichelberger Papers at the Untied States Army Military History Institute at Carlisle Barracks, Pa. Hereafter cited as Eichelberger Dictations (USAMHI).

14. Eichelberger Dictations, 12 September 1958.

15. Ibid.

16. Ibid.

17. Eichelberger Dictations to Virginia C. Westall (undated).

18. Luvaas, *Miss Em*, p. 6.

19. Biographical sketch prepared by Eichelberger for Milton MacKaye, his co-author on *Our Jungle Road to Tokyo* (New York: Viking Press, 1950), 8 February 1948.

20. Eichelberger Dictations, 12 September 1958.

21. Eichelberger Dictations, 25 March 1955; Eichelberger Dictations (undated) to Virginia C. Westall; Anders, *Gentle Knight*, p. 39.

22. Eichelberger Dictations, 25 August 1958.

23. Ibid.

24. Eichelberger Dictations, 25 March 1955.

25. R. L. Eichelberger to Colonel Wirt Robinson, 15 May 1920; Eichelberger Dictations (undated) to Virginia C. Westall.

26. Luvaas, *Miss Em*, p. 7; Eichelberger to Colonel Wirt Robinson, 15 May 1920. Bradley, *General's Life* p. 41.

27. Eichelberger Dictations (USAMHI), 1954; USMA Special Collections.

28. Ibid.

29. Ibid.

30. William A. Williams, "American Intervention in Russia, 1917–1920," *Studies on the Left* III (June 1953): 36.

31. George Kennan, *Russia and the West under Lenin and Stalin* (Boston: Little, Brown, 1960), p. 44; Betty Miller Unterberger, *America's Siberian Expedition, 1918–1920* (Durham, N.C.: Duke University Press, 1956), p. 29.

32. Kennan, *Russia and the West*, p. 100.

33. Unterberger, *Siberian Expedition*, p. 30.

34. Kennan, *Russia and the West*, p. 75.

35. Ibid., p. 97.

36. William S. Graves, *America's Siberian Adventure, 1918–1920* (New York: Jonathan Cape and Harrison Smith, 1931), p. 37.

37. Kennan, *Russia and the West*, p. 105.

38. Eichelberger Dictations (USAMHI), 1954.

39. Eichelberger and MacKaye, *Jungle Road*, p. xiii. Judith Luckett, "Siberia," *Military Review*, April 1984, pp. 58–60.

40. Luvaas, *Miss Em*, p. 11. Kenneth Jolemare, "Mentor," *Military Review*, July 1986, pp. 8–9.

41. Eichelberger Dictations (USAMHI), 1954.

42. Department of the Army, Biographical Sketch of General Eichelberger, dated 28 January 1948, Eichelberger Papers, William R. Perkins Library, Duke University, hereafter cited as Eichelberger Papers, DU. This included the Distinguished Service Cross Citation for 28 June to 3 July 1919.

43. Eichelberger Dictations, 13 October 1954; Eichelberger Dictations of 23 September 1957, contained in Luvaas, *Miss Em,* p. 10.
44. Eichelberger and MacKaye, *Jungle Road,* p. xiv.
45. Major General F. J. Kernan to R. L. Eichelberger, 12 March 1921, Eichelberger Papers, DU; USMA Special Collections Archives.
46. General Graves to R. L. Eichelberger, 8 October 1920, Eichelberger Papers, DU.
47. Eichelberger Dictations (USAMHI), 27 January 1961; and Eichelberger Dictations for Milton MacKaye, 8 February 1948.
48. Colonel S. Heintzelman to R. L. Eichelberger, 12 January 1922, Eichelberger Papers, DU.
49. Major General John L. Hines to R. L. Eichelberger, 24 August 1923, Eichelberger Papers, DU.
50. Russell F. Weigley, *History of the United States Army,* (Louis Morton, general editor, The Macmillan Wars of the United States Series, (New York: Macmillan Company, 1973), p. 400.
51. Russell F. Weigley, *Towards an American Army: Military Thought from Washington to Marshall* (New York: Columbia University Press, 1962), p. 240.
52. Eichelberger Dictations (USAMHI), 27 January 1961.
53. Ibid; USMA Special Collections Archives.
54. *Annual Report of the Commandant: The General Service Schools, 1925–1926* (Fort Leavenworth, Kans.: The General Service Schools Press, 1926), pp. 6–10. Bradley, *A General's Life,* p. 54.
55. Eichelberger Dictations (USAMHI), 27 January 1961. Bradley, *A General's Life,* p. 60.
56. *Annual Report of Commandant,* p. 13.
57. Ibid., p. 11.
58. Ibid., pp. 6–7; and Eichelberger Dictations for Milton MacKaye, 8 February 1948.
59. George Pappas, *Prudens Futuri: The U.S. Army War College, 1901–1967* (Carlisle Barracks, Pa.: Alumni Association of the U.S. Army War College, 1968), p. 136.
60. *U.S. Army War College Directory, 1905–1978* (Carlisle Barracks, Pa.: U.S. Army War College, 1978), pp. 26–27.
61. Eichelberger Dictations (USAMHI), 27 January 1961.
62. Pappas, *Prudens Futuri,* p. 135; USMA Special Collections Archives.
63. Ibid., p. 136. Eichelberger and MacKaye, *Jungle Road,* p. xv.
64. William D. Connor to James F. McKinley, 2 May 1933, Eichelberger Papers, DU.
65. J. F. McKinley to R. L. Eichelberger, 18 September 1934, Eichelberger Papers, DU.

66. Eichelberger Dictations, 28 March 1955.

67. Eichelberger Dictations to Milton MacKaye, 13 February 1948.

68. Weigley, *History of the United States Army,* p. 415; USMA Special Collections.

69. Eichelberger Dictations to Milton MacKaye, 13 February 1948.

70. William D. Connor to AG of the Army, 19 December 1936, Eichelberger Papers, DU.

71. Ibid.

72. Eichelberger Dictations (USAMHI), 27 January 1961.

73. William D. Connor to R. L. Eichelberger, 17 September 1936, Eichelberger Papers, DU.

74. General Simonds to R. L. Eichelberger, 12 September 1936, Eichelberger Papers, DU.

75. Eichelberger Dictations (USAMHI), 27 January 1961.

76. Ibid.; and Eichelberger Dictations (undated), titled "Memorandum on Leadership."

77. Eichelberger Dictations, 25 November 1957.

78. Ibid.

79. Eichelberger Dictations, 31 July 1961; Eichelberger Dictations (undated), titled "Memorandum on Leadership."

80. Eichelberger Dictations for Milton MacKaye, 13 February 1948.

81. Eichelberger Dictations (undated), titled "Memorandum on Leadership."

82. Eichelberger Dictations, 25 November 1957.

83. Ibid.

84. Ibid., and Eichelberger Dictations, 7 December 1954.

85. R. L. Eichelberger to Major General Francis H. Wilby, 21 January 1942, Eichelberger Papers, DU.

86. Eichelberger Dictations, 7 December 1954 and 25 November 1957.

87. *The Superintendent's Annual Report,* 30 June 1941 (West Point Archives).

88. R. L. Eichelberger to General Wilby, 21 January 1942.

89. Eichelberger Dictations, 7 December 1954.

90. Eichelberger and MacKaye, *Jungle Road,* p. xix.

91. Ibid., pp. xix–xx.

92. Ibid., p. xxii; Eichelberger Dictations, 25 November 1957.

93. Eichelberger Dictations for Milton MacKaye, 15 February 1948.

94. Ibid.

95. Max Meyers, *Ours to Hold High: The History of the 77th Infantry Division in World War II* (Washington, D.C.: Infantry Journal Press, 1947), pp. 15–16.

96. Quoted in a letter from General Marshall to Commanding General of the 77th Division, 12 June 1942, Eichelberger Papers, DU.

97. Eichelberger and MacKaye, *Jungle Road*, pp. xxiii–xxv; Eichelberger Dictations, 7 December 1954.

98. Meyers, *Ours to Hold*, p. 18; Eichelberger Dictations for Milton MacKaye, 15 February 1948; Luvaas, *Miss Em*, p. 15; Forrest Pogue, *George C. Marshall Ordeal and Hope*, 3 vols. to date: 1939–1943 (New York: Viking Press, 1963), pp. 334–35.

99. Eichelberger and MacKaye, *Jungle Road*, p. xxvi; Eichelberger Dictations for Milton MacKaye, 15 February 1948.

*Notes to Chapter 2*

1. Eichelberger and MacKaye, *Jungle Road*, pp. 4–5; D. Clayton James, *Years of MacArthur*, pp. 77–80.

2. Trevor DuPuy and R. Ernest DuPuy, *The Encyclopedia of Military History* (New York: Harper & Row, 1970), pp. 1130–41.

3. Milner, *Victory in Papua*, pp. 1, 38–39; Eichelberger and MacKaye, *Jungle Road*, p. 10.

4. Mayo, *Bloody Buna*, pp. 7, 18; War Department, *Papuan Campaign*, p. 2.

5. Eichelberger and MacKaye, *Jungle Road*, pp. 6–7.

6. Eichelberger Dictations, 9 August 1961; Luvaas, *Miss Em*, p. 33.

7. Ibid., June 1948; Eichelberger and MacKaye, *Jungle Road*, pp. 6–7.

8. The Adjutant General's Office, *Official Army Register* (Washington, D.C.: U.S. Government Printing Office, 1946), pp. 72, 101, 439, 587; *Cullum Register of Graduates, 1983*, p. 355.

9. Milner, *Victory in Papua*, p. 50; Eichelberger and MacKaye, *Jungle Road*, p. 22.

10. Bradley, *General's Life*, p. 38.

11. Leslie Anders, *Gentle Knight*, pp. 119–20, 150–74.

12. Eichelberger and MacKaye, *Jungle Road*, p. 63.

13. William McCarthy, *The Jungleers: A History of the 41st Division* (Washington: Infantry Journal Press, 1948), p. 6; Luvaas, "Leavenworth Nightmare," p. 191.

14. Lieutenant Colonel David Larr to General Stephen Chamberlain, 21 May 1942, titled "Training Status of the 41st Division with reference to Preparation for Jungle Warfare," Eichelberger Papers, DU.

15. Ibid.

16. John English, *On Infantry*, pp. 156–60.

17. Milner, *Victory in Papua*, p. 133; Luvaas, "Leavenworth Nightmare," p. 192. Anders, *Gentle Knight*, pp. 208–14.

18. Eichelberger and MacKaye, *Jungle Road*, p. 11; Milner, *Victory*, p. 133.

19. Colonel Russell Reeder to General R. L. Eichelberger, 14 June 1943, Eichelberger Papers, DU.

20. Milner, *Victory*, p. 133; Eichelberger and MacKaye, *Jungle Road*, p. 12. R. L. Eichelberger to Major General V. L. Peterson, 19 January 1943 (not sent), Eichelberger Papers, DU.

21. Milner, *Victory*, p. 56.

22. Ibid.; *Papuan Campaign*, pp. 10–21, 21.

23. James, *Years of MacArthur*, p. 204; Milner, *Victory*, p. 98.

24. *Papuan Campaign*, p. 5.

25. Eichelberger Dictations, 12 November 1954, "Critique of Victory in Papua," Eichelberger Papers, DU; *Papuan Campaign*, p. 13.

26. R. Eichelberger to Major General V. L. Peterson, 19 January 1943 (not sent), Eichelberger Papers, DU.

27. Luvaas, "Leavenworth Nightmare," p. 213; Spector, *Eagle against the Sun*, p. xv; Luvaas, *Miss Em*, p. 16.

28. John I. Alger, *Definitions and Doctrine of the Military Art*, p. 44.

29. E. F. Harding to R. L. Eichelberger, 27 October 1942; Eichelberger Papers, DU.

30. R. Eichelberger to D. MacArthur, 24 December 1942, Eichelberger Papers, DU; Allied Forces, SWPA, "History of Buna," p. 10.

31. *Papuan Campaign*, pp. 14, 16.

32. English, *Infantry*, pp. 157–60; Milner, *Victory*, p. 201.

33. Milner, *Victory*, p. 195; Mayo, *Bloody Buna*, p. 97.

34. Eichelberger Dictations, 9 August 1961, Eichelberger Papers, DU; James, *Years of MacArthur*, p. 243.

35. Mayo, *Bloody Buna*, p. 102; Kenney, *General Kenny Reports*, p. 150.

36. Milner, *Victory*, p. 135.

37. Ibid., p. 191; Anders, *Gentle Knight*, p. 255.

38. *Papuan Campaign*, pp. 12, 16, 24.

39. Kenney, *General Kenny Reports*, p. 134.

40. G. J. Kahn, "The Terrible days of Company E," *Saturday Evening Post*, 15 January 1944, p. 76.

41. R. Eichelberger to K. Sutherland, 9 December 1942, Eichelberger Papers, DU; Milner, *Victory*, p. 203; Anders *Gentle Knight*, p. 229.

42. Anders, *Gentle Knight*, p. 229; Army Register, p. 496.

43. James, *Years of MacArthur*, p. 193.

44. Eichelberger and MacKaye, *Jungle Road*, p. 21.

45. Alger, DDMA, p. 15.

46. Eichelberger and MacKaye, *Jungle Road*, p. 22.

47. Alger, DDMA, p. 5.

48. R. Eichelberger to R. Sutherland, 1 December 1942; R. Eichelberger Diary, 1 December 1942, Eichelberger Papers, DU.

49. Anders, *Gentle Knight,* p. 251.

50. R. Eichelberger to R. Sutherland, 3 December 1942; Eichelberger Diary, 2 December 1942, Eichelberger Papers, DU; Anders, *Gentle Knight,* p. 243.

51. Draft Operations Summary for 2 December 1942 (n.d.) Eichelberger Papers, DU; Eichelberger and MacKaye, *Jungle Road,* p. 25.

52. R. Eichelberger to R. Sutherland, 3 December 1942, Eichelberger Papers, DU.

53. Ibid.; Draft Operations Summary for 2 December 1942 (n.d.); R. Eichelberger to H. Fuller, 14 December 1942, Eichelberger Papers, DU; Milner, *Victory,* p. 207.

54. War Department, "History of Buna," p. 71; Draft Operations Summary, 2 December 1942 (n.d.); R. Eichelberger to H. Fuller, 14 December 1942, Eichelberger Papers, DU.

55. R. Eichelberger to R. Sutherland, 3 December 1942; Eichelberger Diary, 2 December 1942; Draft Operations Summary, 2 December 1942, Eichelberger Papers, DU; Luvaas, "Leavenworth Nightmare," p. 211.

56. R. Eichelberger to R. Sutherland, 3 and 4 December 1942, Eichelberger Papers, DU; *Cullum Register of Graduates,* p. 313.

57. Eichelberger and MacKaye, *Jungle Road,* pp. 26–28; Milner, *Victory,* pp. 234–235; R. Eichelberger to V. L. Peterson, 19 January 1943, Eichelberger Papers, DU.

58. Milner, *Victory,* p. 235; War Department, "History of Buna," p. 73.

59. R. Eichelberger to R. Sutherland, 3–5 December 1945; Eichelberger Diary, 3–5 December 1942, Eichelberger Papers, DU; Milner, *Victory,* pp. 242–45; Eichelberger and MacKaye, *Jungle Road,* pp. 28–31; Luvaas, *Miss Em,* p. 40.

60. Eichelberger Diary, 6–14 December 1942; R. Eichelberger to R. Sutherland, 6–8 December 1942, Eichelberger Papers, DU; Milner, *Victory,* p. 261.

61. Milner, *Victory,* p. 255.

62. Ibid., p. 245; Memorandum on Night Patrolling, 12 December 1942 (RG407: 332–INF(127–0.8), Federal Records Center, Suitland, Md.; Alger, *DDMA,* p. 89; Eichelberger and MacKaye, *Jungle Road,* pp. 26–27; Fred Brown to R. Eichelberger, 4 August 1961, Eichelberger Papers, DU.

63. D. MacArthur to R. Eichelberger, 14 December 1942, Eichelberger Papers, DU.

64. R. Eichelberger to R. Sutherland, 15 December 1942, Eichelberger Papers, DU.

65. Ibid., 13 December 1942; R. Eichelberger to E. Eichelberger, 14 December 1942, Eichelberger Papers, DU.

66. D. MacArthur to R. Eichelberger, 13 December 1942; Eichelberger Dictations, 12 November 1954, Eichelberger Papers, DU.

67. D. MacArthur to R. Eichelberger, 25 December 1942, Eichelberger Papers, DU.
68. R. Eichelberger to V. Peterson, 19 January 1943; Eichelberger Dictations, 12 November 1954, Eichelberger Papers, DU; *Papuan Campaign*, p. 57.
69. R. Eichelberger to R. Sutherland, 16, 19, 20, 22, 26 December 1942; R. Eichelberger to E. Eichelberger, 15 December 1942, Eichelberger Papers, DU.
70. R. G. 407: 332–INF(127)–0.8, December 1942–January 1943, "Diary of Suganuma," Federal Records Center, Suitland, Md.
71. *Papuan Campaign*, p. 44.
72. R. Eichelberger to V. Peterson, 19 January 1943; Eichelberger Memorandum for File: "Chain of Command During the Buna-Sanananda Campaign," 13 May 1943, Eichelberger Papers, DU.
73. R. Eichelberger to R. Sutherland, 12 January 1943; R. Eichelberger to H. Fuller, 14, 22 December 1942; Eichelberger Papers, DU.
74. Luvaas, *Miss Em*, pp. 65–66; James, *Years of MacArthur*, pp. 274–75; *New York Times*, 9 January 1943, p. 4; R. Eichelberger to Colonel Gordon Rogers, 16 October 1943, Eichelberger Papers, DU.

*Notes to Chapter 3*

1. Eichelberger and MacKaye, *Jungle Road*, pp. 63–64; Luvaas, *Miss Em*, pp. 60–67.
2. R. Eichelberger to E. Eichelberger, 22 October 1943, Eichelberger Papers, DU.
3. Clyde Eddleman Papers, Military History Institute, Carlisle Barracks, Pa.; Colonel Charles Schilling to Major General James Lampert, 10 May 1966.
4. Eichelberger and MacKaye, *Jungle Road*, p. 47; James, *Years of MacArthur*, p. 278.
5. R. Eichelberger to E. Eichelberger, 22 October 1943; R. Eichelberger to Major General V. L. Peterson, 19 January 1943, Eichelberger Papers, DU; Luvaas, *Miss Em*, p. 62.
6. Memorandum entitled "Losses in Papua Low: Review in GHQ Communique," 29 January 1943; D. MacArthur to R. Eichelberger 13 and 25 December 1942; Eichelberger Dictations, 9 September 1953; R. Eichelberger to E. Eichelberger, 22 October 1943, Eichelberger Papers, DU; Luvaas, *Miss Em*, p. 63; James, *Years of MacArthur*, p. 281.
7. James, *Years of MacArthur*, p. 281.
8. Eichelberger Dictations, 9 September 1953, Eichelberger Papers, DU.

9. Ibid., 11 January 1954; Luvaas, *Miss Em*, p. 65.

10. R. Eichelberger to Major General Alec Surles, 21 October 1943; W. Connor to R. Eichelberger, 31 October 1943, Eichelberger Papers, DU; Luvaas, *Miss Em*, p. 65.

11. R. Eichelberger to E. Eichelberger, 13 January 1944, Eichelberger Papers, DU; Luvaas, *Miss Em*, p. 88.

12. Martin Van Creveld, *Fighting Power* (London: Arms and Armour Press, 1983), p. 112; Robert Manning, ed., *Above and Beyond: A History of the Medal of Honor* (Boston: Boston Publishing Company, 1985), p. 3.

13. R. Eichelberger to E. Eichelberger, 22 October 1943; R. Eichelberger to C. Fenton, 20 October 1943, Eichelberger Papers, DU.

14. R. Eichelberger to E. Eichelberger, 22 October 1943, Eichelberger Papers, DU; Luvaas, *Miss Em*, pp. 69, 84.

15. R. Eichelberger to C. Fenton, 20 October 1943, Eichelberger Papers, DU; Luvaas, *Miss Em*, p. 69.

16. R. Eichelberger to D. MacArthur, 24 December 1942, and R. Eichelberger to E. Eichelberger, 25 April 1943, Eichelberger Papers, DU.

17. R. Eichelberger, Address to the Twenty-fourth Division, October 1943, Eichelberger Papers, DU.

18. R. Eichelberger to W. Krueger, 19 July 1943, Eichelberger Papers, DU.

19. Colonel Frank S. Bowen to R. Eichelberger, 18 February 1943, Eichelberger Papers, DU.

20. Brigadier General Richard Tindall, "Initiative" (1937), *The Infantry Journal Reader*, ed. Joseph Green, (Garden City, N.Y.: Doubleday, Doran & Co., 1943), pp. 316–17.

21. R. Eichelberger to H. Fuller, 14, 22 December 1942, Eichelberger Papers, DU.

22. Rex Chandler to O. Chandler, 18 May 1943, Rex Chandler Papers, World War II Miscellaneous Collections, Archives, U.S. Military History Institute; Cullum Collection, West Point Archives; FM 100–5 (1986), p. 15.

23. Report of the Commanding General Buna Forces on the Buna Campaign: 1 December 1942–25 January 1943, pp. 72–73. Eichelberger Papers, DU.

24. Colonel Frank Bowen to R. Eichelberger, 5 February 1944, titled, "Status of Training in I Corps,"; ibid., 18 February 1944, Also to understand fully Eichelberger's training philosophy, I used Eighth Army Training Memorandum No. 1, 1 October 1944, which was published by Eichelberger after the Hollandia operation. Eichelberger Papers, DU; NYE, *The Challenge of Command*, p. 84.

25. Colonel Frank Bowen to R. Eichelberger, 18 February 1944; Eighth

Army Training Memorandum No. 1, 1 October 1944, Eichelberger Papers, DU; Luvaas, "Leavenworth Nightmare," p. 192; FM 22–100 (1983), pp. 78–79.

26. R. Eichelberger to E. Eichelberger, 24 January 1944 and 21 August 1943; "History of I Corps," p. 17, Eichelberger Papers, DU.; Luvaas, *Miss Em*, pp. 66, 89.

27. Allied Forces, Southwest Pacific area, "The 24th Division History of the Hollandia Operation," p. 37, Eichelberger Papers, DU; James, *Years of MacArthur*, p. 310; Alger, *DDMA*, p. 12; *FM 100–5*, p. 101; Smith, *Approach*, p. 3.

28. "The 24th Division History of Hollandia," p. 37, Eichelberger Papers, DU; Eichelberger and MacKaye, *Jungle Road*, pp. 95–96, 101; James, *Years of MacArthur*, p. 338.

29. Eichelberger and MacKaye, *Jungle Road*, p. 101; Smith, *Approach*, p. 9; "24th Division History of Hollandia," p. 37.

30. Russell F. Weigley, *The American Way of War: A History of United States Military Strategy and Policy, The Wars of the United States Series*, Louis Milton, gen. ed. (Bloomington: Indiana University Press, 1973), p. 281; Maurice Mittoff, *Strategic Planning for Coalition Warfare, 1943–1944*, (Washington, D.C.: Office of the Chief of Military History, Department of the Army, 1959), p. 5, citing interview, Major Roy Lanson and Major David Hamilton with General Marshall, 23 July 1949, OCMH files; Smith, *Approach*, p. 12.

31. "24th Division History of Hollandia," p. 26; James, *Years of MacArthur*, p. 445; Smith, *Approach*, pp. 9, 13.

32. Ibid.

33. James, *Years of MacArthur*, pp. 444–45, Smith, *Approach*, p. 13.

34. RG 407: 201–0.3: B. 3022. "Report on Operations of I corps at Hollandia," by Colonel Edwin Carns, 26 May 1944, p. 3, National Research Center, Suitland, Md., hereafter cited as "Carns Report"; Eichelberger and MacKaye, *Jungle Road*, p. 105.

35. Allied Forces, "I Corps History of the Hollandia Operation," p. 1; Allied Forces, "24th Division at Hollandia," p. 39, Eichelberger Papers, DU; Record Group 407: 201–0.1–B.3017 "History of I Corps," p. 18, National Research Center, Suitland, Md., hereafter cited as "History of I Corps."

36. Allied forces, "History of the 24th Division at Hollandia," p. 40, Eichelberger Papers, DU.

37. FM 100–5, p. 97; R. Eichelberger to E. Eichelberger 31 March 1945, Eichelberger Papers, DU.

38. Cullum Files, West Point Archives; Eichelberger and MacKaye, *Jungle Road*, p. 104.

39. Allied Forces, "I Corps History of Hollandia," p. 3, Eichelberger Papers, DU.

40. "Carns Report" pp. 3–4, National Records Center, Suitland, Md., hereafter cited as Carns Report; RG 407: 324 Inf. (21)–0.3 B. 7943, "Narrated Events 21st Inf. Opn," p. 1, National Records Center, Suitland, Md.; Eichelberger Diary, 8 April 1944, Eichbelberger Papers, DU.

41. Smith, *Approach*, pp. 42–43; Eichelberger and MacKaye, *Jungle Road*, p. 106.

42. Eichelberger Diary, 22 April 1944; Allied Forces, "I Corps History of Hollandia," p. 10, Eichelberger Papers, DU; Eichelberger and MacKaye, *Jungle Road*, p. 106.

43. Allied Forces, "I Corps History of Hollandia," p. 5, Eichelberger Papers, DU; Smith, *Approach*, p. 57.

44. Cullum Collection, USMA Archives, West Point, N.Y.

45. Allied Forces, "I Corps History of Hollandia," p. 6, Eichelberger Papers, DU; Smith, *Approach*, p. 58–60; Eichelberger and MacKaye, *Jungle Road*, pp. 108–109.

46. RG 407: 201–0.3: B.3022 "Report on Operations of I corps at Hollandia," by Colonel Edwin Carns, 26 May 1944, p. 1, National Records Center, Suitland, Md., hereafter cited as "Carns Report"; Smith, *Approach*, p. 60; Allied Forces, "I Corps History of Hollandia," p. 6, Eichelberger Papers, DU; Cullum Collection, USMA Archives, West Point, N.Y.

47. Smith, *Approach*, p. 58.

48. James, *Years of MacArthur*, p. 452; Eichelberger Dictations, 12 November 1954, Eichelberger Papers, DU.

49. Alger, *DDMA*, p. 163; Eichelberger Dictations, 12 November 1954; Eichelberger Diary, 22 April 1944, Eichelberger Papers, DU.

50. Daniel Barbey, *MacArthur's Amphibious Navy: Seventh Amphibious Force Operations, 1943–1945* (Annapolis, Md.: United States Naval Institute, 1969), p. 73, quoted in Luvaas, *Miss Em*, p. 142.

51. Eichelberger and MacKaye, *Jungle Road*, p. 109; Smith, *Approach*, p. 76.

52. Smith, *Approach*, pp. 76, 83, 84, 99–101; Eichelberger and MacKaye, *Jungle Road*, p. 110.

53. Eichelberger and MacKaye, *Jungle Road*, pp. 113–14.

54. Ibid.; Eichelberger Diary, 28 April–6 June 1944; Clovis Byers to E. Eichelberger, 30 May 1944; Allied Forces, "24th Division History of Hollandia," p. 117, Eichelberger Papers, DU; Smith, *Approach*, p. 83.

55. Eichelberger Diary, 2, 15 May 1944, Eichelberger Papers, DU; FM 22–100, p. 222.

56. R. Eichelberger to E. Eichelberger, 15 May 1944; Luvaas, *Miss Em*, p. 114; Forrest C. Pogue, *George C. Marshall: Organizer of Victory*, vol. 3 (New York: Viking Press, 1973), p. 442; James, *Years of MacArthur*, p. 453.

57. Kenney, *General Kenney Reports*, p. 289; James, *Years of MacArthur*, p. 459; Luvaas, *Miss Em*, p. 125.

58. James, *Years of MacArthur*, pp. 453, 458; Spencer Davis, "Slaughter at Biak," *Australia Newsweek*, 12 June 1944, Eichelberger Papers, DU; RG 407–201–2: B.3028, "G–2 Summary of the Biak Operation: 27 May–29 June 1944," p. 2, Federal Research Center, Suitland, Md., hereafter cited as "G–2 Summary of Biak."

59. "G–2 Summary of Biak," pp. 2–4, 7–9; Smith, *Approach*, p. 299.

60. Ibid., p. 4.

61. Ibid., p. 5; Davis, "Slaughter at Biak," 12 June 1944, Eichelberger Papers, DU; Eichelberger and MacKaye, *Jungle Road*, p. 139; Smith, *Approach*, p. 325.

62. Smith, *Approach*, p. 91.

63. James, *Years of MacArthur*, pp. 459–60; Davis, "Slaughter at Biak," 12 June 1944, Eichelberger Papers, DU.

64. James, *Years of MacArthur*, pp. 459–60.

65. Krueger, *Down Under*, p. 101; Riegelman, *Caves of Biak*, p. 138; Smith, *Approach*, p. 342; Kenneth Sweany to Hargis Westerfield, 9 October 1978, Hargis Westerfield Collection, OCMH, MHI.

66. Allied Forces, "I Corps History of the Biak Operation," p. 3; Eichelberger Diary, 14 June 1944, Eichelberger Papers, DU.

67. Eichelberger Diary, 15 June 1944, Eichelberger Papers, DU; Kenneth Sweany to Hargis Westerfield, 9 October 1978, Hargis Westerfield Collection, OCMH, MHI.

68. Eichelberger Diary, 15 June 1944; R. Eichelberger to W. Krueger, 16 June 1944, Eichelberger Papers, DU.

69. W. Krueger to R. Eichelberger, 17 June 1944, Eichelberger Papers, DU; Eichelberger and MacKaye, *Jungle Road*, p. 146.

70. Allied Forces, "History of the Biak Operation," pp. 5–6, Eichelberger Papers, DU; Smith, *Approach*, pp. 368–69.

71. Eichelberger and MacKaye, *Jungle Road*, p. 146.

72. R. Eichelberger to E. Eichelberger, 19 June 1944, Eichelberger Papers, DU; Riegelman, *Caves of Biak*, p. 142.

73. Smith, *Approach*, p. 372; Eichelberger and MacKaye, *Jungle Road*, p. 150.

74. Eichelberger Diary, 19 June 1944; Allied Forces, "History of the Biak Operation," p. 8, Eichelberger Papers, DU.

75. James, *Years of MacArthur*, p. 460.

## Notes to Chapter 4

1. Eichelberger and MacKaye, *Jungle Road*, p. 157.
2. "Report of the Commanding General, Eighth Army on the Mindanao Operation" (page not numbered); Eichelberger Dictations, 29 August 1955, Eichelberger Papers, DU.
3. R. Eichelberger to E. Eichelberger, 30 June 1944, in Luvaas, *Miss Em*, pp. 140–41; Eichelberger and MacKaye, *Jungle Road*, pp. 157.
4. R. Eichelberger to E. Eichelberger, 21 August 1944, in Luvaas, *Miss Em*, p. 151; Eichelberger and MacKaye, *Jungle Road*, p. 157; W. Krueger to D. MacArthur, 2 July 1944, Krueger Papers, USMA Archives, West Point, N.Y.
5. Weigley, *Eisenhower's Lieutenants*, p. 662; Eichelberger Dictations, 29 August 1955, Eichelberger Papers, DU.
6. Krueger notes on MacArthur, p. 29, Krueger Papers, USMA Archives, West Point, N.Y.; Eichelberger Dictations, 29 August 1955; R. Eichelberger to E. Eichelberger, 8 September 1944 Eichelberger Papers, DU.
7. R. Eichelberger to E. Eichelberger, 15 October 1944, in Luvaas, *Miss Em*, p. 160; R. Eichelberger to D. MacArthur, 15 February 1945, Eichelberger Papers, DU.
8. Interview with General John R. Jannarone, 6 November 1984, at the United States Military Academy, West Point, N.Y.; John R. Jannarone in the Cullum Files, Association of Graduates, West Point, N.Y.
9. MacArthur, *Reminiscences*, pp. 210–11; General Order No. 3, Headquarters, Eighth Army, 7 September 1944, Eichelberger Papers, DU.
10. Robert Eichelberger, "The Amphibious Eighth" (n.p., n.d.), p. 2, Eichelberger Papers, DU; James, *MacArthur*, p. 499.
11. Eighth Army, Training Directive No. 1, 1 October 1944 (Enclosure 1), pp. 1–11, Eichelberger Papers, DU.
12. Eighth Army Training Directive No. 1, p. 11; "A Report of the Command General Eighth Army—Leyte Samar Operation, 26 December 1944 to 8 May 1945," p. 32, Eichelberger Papers, DU.
13. R. Eichelberger to E. Eichelberger, 19–20 November 1944; Eichelberger, "The Amphibious Eighth," p. 2, Eichelberger Papers, DU.
14. M. Hamlin Cannon, *Leyte: The Return to the Philippines* (Washington, D.C.: Department of the Army, Office of the Chief of Military History, 1954), pp. 10–11.
15. Ibid., pp. 21, 26, 102, 367–68; Douglas MacArthur, *Reports of General MacArthur: The Campaigns of MacArthur in the Pacific*, vol. 1. (Washington, D.C.: Department of the Army, 1966), pp. 226, 237;

"C. G. Report Leyte-Samar," p. 2, Eichelberger Papers, DU; James, *MacArthur*, p. 602.

16. Spector, *Eagle against the Sun*, p. 517; R. Eichelberger to E. Eichelberger, 27 November 1944, Luvaas, *Miss Em*, p. 172. R. Eichelberger to E. Eichelberger, 8–9 December 1944, Eichelberger Papers, DU.

17. Eichelberger Dictations, 21 June 1955, Eichelberger Papers, DU; Eichelberger and MacKaye, *Jungle Road*, p. 181; "C. G. Report Leyte-Samar," pp. 7, 16.

18. R. Eichelberger to E. Eichelberger, 25 January 1945, Eichelberger Papers, DU; *New York Times*, 12 June 1945, p. 2; Eichelberger and MacKaye, *Jungle Road*, p. 182.

19. Eichelberger and MacKaye, *Jungle Road*, p. 182; "C. G. Report Leyte-Samar," p. 17, Eichelberger Papers, DU.

20. FM 100–5 (1986), pp. 60–61; Memorandum entitled "Logistical Problems of the Eighth Army at Peak Load, January 1945," pp. 1–2; Eichelberger Papers, DU.

21. Max Meyers, *Ours to Hold High: The History of the 77th Division in World War II* (Washington, D.C.: Infantry Journal Press, 1947), p. 182; Eichelberger Diary, 1, 2, 4, 19, 22, 25 January 1945, Eichelberger Papers, DU.

22. Walter Krueger, Lecture to the Command and General Staff College, 20 May 1952, entitled "Field Army Operations," Krueger Papers, West Point, N.Y.; Smith, *Triumph*, pp. 88–96. James, *MacArthur*, p. 625.

23. Smith, *Triumph*, pp. 95–97, 242–43.

24. Krueger, "Field Army Operations," Krueger Papers, West Point, N.Y.

25. Krueger, "Douglas MacArthur," Krueger Papers, West Point, N.Y.; Eichelberger Dictations, 4 November 1960, Eichelberger Papers, DU; Walter Krueger, *From Down Under to Nippon*, pp. 218, 225–28.

26. Eichelberger Diary, 23 January and 23 March 1945, Eichelberger Papers, DU; Smith, *Triumph*, p. 212; James, *MacArthur*, p. 631.

27. "Historical Report Luzon Campaign, XI Corps," p. 3, RG 407: 211.–0.3 Box 4159 XI Corps Supporting Document for After Action Reports, 14 November 1944–13 June 1945, National Research Center, Suitland, Md.; "11th Airborne Division History of the Luzon Operation," 3 August 1945, p. 1. RG 407: 311–0 Box 7582, National Research Center, Suitland, Md.; Smith, *Triumph*, p. 312; "C. G. Report on Nasugbu and Bataan," p. 75; Craven and Cate, *Air Forces*, p. 422.

28. Charles Hall Biography in Cullum File, USMA, West Point, N.Y.; R. Eichelberger to E. Eichelberger, 29 January 1945; Luvaas, *Miss Em*, p.

204; "C. G. Report on Nasugbu and Bataan," p. 81, Eichelberger Papers, DU.

29. "C. G. Report on Nasugbu and Bataan," pp. 8, 14; "Amphibious Eighth," p. 4, Eichelberger Papers, DU; Smith, *Triumph*, p. 222; "Report after Action with the Enemy Operation Mike VI, Luzon Campaign, 31 January–30 June 1945, p. 3, RG 407: 7.311–0.3 Box 7583, National Records Center, Suitland, Md., hereafter cited as "Operation Shoestring."

30. Edward Flanagan, *The Los Banos Raid* (Novato, Calif: Presidio Press, 1986), pp. 47, 116–17. Eichelberger Dictations, 4 November 1960, Eichelberger Papers, DU; Joseph Swing, in Cullum Papers, West Point, N.Y.

31. Eichelberger Diary, 26–27 January 1945; Eichelberger Dictations, 3 October 1960, Eichelberger Papers, DU.

32. "Operation Shoestring," p. 1; Eichelberger and MacKaye, *Jungle Road*, p. 190.

33. Eichelberger Diary, 31 January 1945; "C. G. Report on Nasugbu and Bataan," Foreword Eichelberger Papers, DU; R. Eichelberger to E. Eichelberger, 20 June 1944, Luvaas, *Miss Em*, p. 133.

34. "Operation Shoestring," p. 1; "C. G. Report on Nasugbu and Bataan," pp. 6, 16, Eichelberger Papers, DU.

35. Eichelberger and MacKaye, *Jungle Road*, p. 190; R. Eichelberger to E. Eichelberger, 2 February 1945, Luvaas, *Miss Em*, p. 208; "Operation Shoestring," p. 2; "C. G. Report on Nasugbu-Bataan," p. 16, Eichelberger Papers, DU.

36. "Operation Shoestring," p. 2; "C. G. Report on Nasugbu-Bataan," pp. 6, 16, Eichelberger Papers, DU; Eichelberger and MacKaye, *Jungle Road*, p. 194.

37. "Operation Shoestring," pp. 2–3; Eichelberger Diary, 3 February 1945, Eichelberger Papers, DU; Flanagan, *Raid*, pp. 58–59, 120; Orin Haugen, Cullum Files, West Point, N.Y.

38. "Operation Shoestring," p. 3; "C. G. Report on Nasugbu-Bataan," p. 22 Eichelberger Papers, DU.

39. Eichelberger Diary, 4 February 1945. "C. G. Report on Nasugbu-Bataan," p. 22, Eichelberger Papers, DU.

40. "Operation Shoestring," p. 4; "C. G. Report on Nasugbu-Bataan," p. 22, Eichelberger Papers, DU.

41. Eichelberger Diary, 4 February 1945; "C. G. Report on Nasugbu-Bataan," pp. 22–24, Eichelberger Papers, DU; "Operation Shoestring," pp. 4–5; Smith, *Triumph*, p. 265; Flanagan, *Raid*, pp. 62–63.

42. "C. G. Report on Nasugbu-Bataan," Foreword; Eichelberger Dictations, 4 November 1960; Major General Dunkel to R. Eichelberger,

3 March 1945, Eichelberger Papers, DU; James, *MacArthur*, pp. 632–34.

43. Eichelberger Diary, 14, 21 February, 3 March 1945; Eichelberger Papers, DU.

44. Eichelberger Dictations, 2 January 1953; Eichelberger Diary, 5 February 1945, Eichelberger Papers, DU; Eichelberger and MacKaye, *Jungle Road*, p. 205; Smith, *Triumph*, p. 364; James, *MacArthur*, p. 671; Craven and Cate, *Air Forces*, p. 450; Spector, *Eagle against the Sun*, p. 526.

45. "Robert Eichelberger, Biographical Summary, 28 January 1948," p. 4; R. Eichelberger to E. Eichelberger, 3 April 1945, Eichelberger Papers, DU; Eichelberger and MacKaye, Jungle Road, p. 202; Spector, *Eagle Against the Sun*, p. 527; Krueger, "Field Army Operations," Krueger Papers, West Point, N.Y.

46. Eichelberger Diary, 13 March 1945; R. Eichelberger to E. Eichelberger, 3 April 1945, Eichelberger Papers, DU.

47. "Report of the Commanding General Eighth Army on the Palawan, Zamboanga Operations," p. 5.

48. Eichelberger Diary, 21, 27, 28 February 1945; "Report of the C. G. Palwan-Zamboanga," p. 11, Eichelberger Papers, DU; Memorandum, "Report on Victor III Operation, 2 April 1945," Captain C. E. Arnold to Colonel Frank Bowen. RG 407: 7.18–3.01 Box 2770, NRC, Suitland, Md.

49. "C. G. Report on Palawan-Zamboanga," pp. 12–16; Eichelberger Papers, DU; Smith, *Triumph*, p. 589.

50. "C. G. Report on Palawan and Zamboanga," pp. 49, 55; Eichelberger Diary, 9–10 March 1945; "Amphibious Eighth," p. 7; Eichelberger Papers, DU; Smith, *Triumph*, p. 596.

51. "C. G. Report on Panay, Negros and Cebu Operations," pp. 1, 22, 25, 27; Eichelberger Diary, 13, 23 March 1945; "Amphibious Eighth," p. 7; Eichelberger Dictations, 2 January 1953, Eichelberger Papers, DU.

52. Eichelberger Diary, 23 March 1945, Eichelberger Papers, DU.

53. Ibid., 30, 31 March 1945; R. Eichelberger to E. Eichelberger, 31 March 1945; "C. G. Report on Panay and Negros," pp. 16, 18, 27, 30, 33; "Amphibious Eighth," pp. 7–8, Eichelberger Papers, DU; Captain James Barron to Colonel Frank Bowen, 1 April 1945, memorandum entitled: "Report on the Taking of Bago River Bridge on 29 March 1945." RG 407: 7.108–3.01 Box 2770, NRC, Suitland, Md.

54. "C. G. Report on Panay-Negros," pp. 35, 44. Eichelberger Papers, DU.

55. Clovis Byers memorandum: "Interview with General MacArthur, Saturday, 30 March 1945," Eichelberger Papers, DU.

56. "C. G. Report Panay, Negros, Cebu," pp. 61–74; "Amphibious Eighth," p. 8; Eichelberger Diary, 26 March 1945; Eichelberger Papers,

DU; Eichelberger and MacKaye, *Jungle Road*, pp. 214–15; FM 100–5, p. 95; William Arnold, in Cullum Files, West Point, N.Y.

57. D. MacArthur to R. Eichelberger, 21 April 1945, Eichelberger Papers, DU.

58. Clovis Byers memorandum: "Interview with General MacArthur, Saturday, 30 March 1945"; Eichelberger Diary 8–10 April 1945; Eichelberger Papers, DU.

59. Eichelberger Diary, 10 April 1945, Eichelberger Papers, DU.

60. GHQ Communique issued 2230 hours, 20 April 1945; "Report of the Commanding General on the Mindanao Operation," p. 17, Eichelberger Papers, DU.

61. "Report of the Commanding General Eighth Army on the Mindanao Operation," pp. 2–9, 17. Eichelberger Papers, DU; Roscoe Woodruff, "A Narrative Account of the 24th Infantry Division on Mindanao" (n.p., n.d.), p. 2, RG 407: 324–03 Box 7670, National Research Center, Suitland, Md.

62. "Amphibious Eighth," p. 10, Eichelberger Papers, DU; Bradley, *A Soldier's Life*, pp. 223–24; Luvaas, *Miss Em*, pp. 197, 303; Cullum Files, West Point, N.Y.

63. "C. G. Report on Mindanao," pp. 20–24; Eichelberger Diary, 17 April 1945, Eichelberger Papers, DU; "24th Division on Mindanao," p. 2–3, NRC, Suitland, Md.

64. "C. G. Report on Mindanao," p. 28. "24th Division on Mindanao," pp. 3–5; Eichelberger, "Amphibious Eighth," pp. 10–11; "History of X Corps on Mindanao, 17 April 1945–30 June 1945," pp. 19–22. RG 407: 210–0 Box 4107, NRC, Suitland, Md.

65. Eichelberger Diary, 28 April 1945; "C. G. Report on Mindanao," p. 36, Eichelberger Papers, DU; Eichelberger and MacKaye, *Jungle Road*, p. 223.

66. "C. G. Report on Mindanao," p. 48; "24th Division Report on Mindanao," p. 7.

67. "C. G. Report on Mindanao," p. 79; R. Eichelberger to Sue Eichelberger Zerbe, 29 April 1945, Eichelberger Papers, DU.

68. Eichelberger Diary, 3 June 1945; Eichelberger Dictations, 6 March 1961, Eichelberger Papers, DU.

69. "Report of the Commanding General on the Luzon Mop-up," p. 3, 9. Eichelberger Papers, DU; Smith, *Triumph*, pp. 572–73.

70. Eichelberger, "Amphibious Eighth," (cover sheet), Eichelberger Papers, DU; G. Patton to R. Eichelberger, 25 May 1945, in Luvaas, *Miss Em*, p. 24.

## Notes to Epilogue

1. Eichelberger, "The Amphibious Eighth Takes Over," Eichelberger Papers, DU.
2. Eichelberger Dictations, 29 May 1961, Eichelberger Papers, DU.
3. Ibid., 15 June 1959.
4. Ibid. Professor Jay Luvaas to the author, 6 January 1984.

# INDEX

Admiralty Islands, 74, 98, 102
Afrika Corps, 35
Aitape, 85
Alexander of Macedonia, 43
Americal Division, 114, 117, 119, 120
Arnold, William, 117, 119, 120
Asia Atoll, 99

Bacolod, 118, 119
Bago River, 118, 119
Baker, Newton, 10
Barbey, Daniel, 81, 82, 85
Bataan, ix, 34, 43, 104, 106, 113
Bataan Gang, ix, 55, 60, 113, 125
Bernhardt, Sarah, 68
Biak, 82, 83, 84, 85, 86, 87, 88, 89, 91,
    92, 94, 95, 109, 116
Blaik, Earl, 27, 28
Bohol, 114, 117, 120
Bongao Islands, 116
Bougainville, 74, 119
Bowen, Frank, 37, 96, 97, 114, 128
Bradley, Omar, 8, 18, 37, 52, 68, 93,
    107, 122, 129
Brisbane (Australia), 36
Brooke, Alan, 29
Brush, Rapp, 117, 119, 120
Buna, x, xi, 35, 36, 40, 41, 42, 43, 44,
    45, 46, 47, 48, 49, 50, 51, 52, 53, 54,
    55, 56, 57, 58, 59, 60, 61, 62, 63, 64,
    65, 66, 67, 68, 69, 70, 72, 73, 74, 76,
    77, 78, 82, 83, 87, 89, 90, 91, 92, 94,
    95, 96, 99, 105, 109, 113, 115, 117,
    121, 123, 126
Butler, Frederick, 22
Byers, Clovis, 36, 37, 57, 59, 81, 96,
    97, 114, 119, 128, 129

Cape Gloucester, 72
Carns, Edwin, 80
Carranza, Venus Tiono, 8
Cebu, 114, 117, 119, 120, 126
Chamberlin, Stephen, 108
Chandler, Oscar, 72
Chandler, Rex, 72
Churchill, Winston S., 29, 30
Clark Field, 70
Clarkson, Gordon, 56
Clifford, Thomas E., 79, 80, 81, 82
Coolidge, Calvin, 17
Connor, William D., 20, 21, 22, 23, 66
Coral Sea, Battle of, 30, 34
Corregidor, 34
Craig, Malin, 21, 22, 23, 24, 25, 27, 30
Cyclops Mountains (New Guinea), 75

Davao Gulf, 121, 122, 123, 124, 125,
    126

# Index

Davis, Robert C., 18, 19, 23, 30
Davis, Spencer, 87
Davies, Thomas, 8
Decker, George, 81
Devers, Jacob, 3, 22, 91
Digos (Mindanao), 124
Dill, John, 29
Doe, Jens, 88, 89, 115, 116, 120
Dunckel, William, 112

Eddleman, Clyde, 63, 81, 87
Edwards, Daniel K., 53, 59
Egeberg, Roger, 50
Eichelberger, Emma Ring (mother), 1
Eichelberger, George (father), 1
Eichelberger, Robert: physical
    appearance, x; military education, 3,
    18, 19; Siberia, 11–15; leadership
    philosophy 28, 29, 71, 72, 84;
    retirement 127–130
Eichelberger, Mrs. Robert, 1, 7, 101
Eighth Army, 91, 93, 94, 95, 96, 97, 98,
    99, 101, 102, 103, 106, 107, 113, 114,
    115, 116, 117, 120, 121, 124, 125,
    126, 127, 128, 129
Eighth Division, 11, 29
Eighty-second division, 107
Eisenhower, Dwight D., 18, 19, 23, 52,
    93, 107, 122, 127, 128, 129
Eleventh Airborne Division, 107, 108,
    109, 110, 111, 112, 113, 125, 127
Eleventh Corps, 106

Finschafen, 74
First Army (Australian), 36
First Army (U.S.), 68
First Cavalry Division, 96, 113
Foch, Ferdinand, 11
Fortieth Division, 105, 114, 117, 118,
    119
Forty-first Division, 33, 37, 38, 41, 44,
    47, 59, 62, 69, 74, 76, 77, 78, 79, 81,
    82, 85, 86, 87, 88, 89, 90, 91, 114,
    115, 116, 117
Forty-third Division, 105
Forty-third Infantry Regiment, 9, 31
Fourteenth Corps, 105
Freeman, Douglas S., 65
Fuller, Horace, 37, 59, 62, 71, 77, 78,
    79, 81, 82, 84; 85, 86, 87, 88

Geelvink Bay (Biak), 76
Genko Line, 112

Gerow, Leonard, 18
Gona, 35, 40, 41, 42
Gorgas, William, 6
Gowen, James, 4, 5, 18, 30
Graves, William, 9, 10, 11, 13, 14, 16,
    30
Grose, John, 52
Guadalcanal, 40
Guam, 33
Gudger, Emma. See Eichelberger, Mrs.
    Robert L.
Gudger, H. A., 7, 9

Hale, J. Tracey, 46, 49
Hall, Charles, 106
Haney, Harold, 115
Hannibal, 43
Hansa Bay, 75, 76
Hanson, Aaron, 118
Harding, Edwin F., 8, 37, 39, 43, 44,
    45, 46, 47, 48, 49, 50, 51, 52, 54
Harding, Warren, 17
Haugen, Orin, 107, 110, 111
Herring, Edmund, 41, 48, 53, 54, 58,
    67
Hines, John, 17
Hollandia, 75, 76, 77, 78, 79, 80, 81,
    82, 83, 84, 85, 91, 92, 95, 96, 122
Homma, Masaharu, 33, 34
Hopkins, R., 48
Horii, Tomitaro, 35, 40, 41
Humboldt Bay, 75, 77, 79, 81, 82, 83

I Corps, 29, 30, 36, 37, 42, 51, 73, 80,
    83, 95, 96, 98, 99, 104
Illana Gulf, 123
Iloilo, 117
Imus (Luzon), 111
Inada, Masazumi, 83
Inchon, 75
Infantry Journal, 37
Irving, Frederick, 77, 78, 80, 81, 82,
    84, 95, 122
Iwabuchi, Sanji, 104

Jannarone, John, 97, 98
Jolo Islands, 116

Kemper Military Academy, 9
Kenney, George, ix, 45, 47, 50, 113
Kernan, Francis, 16, 30
Kolchak, Aleksandr, 13
Krueger, Walter, 38, 63, 67, 71, 73, 76,

# Index

81, 87, 88, 89, 93, 94, 95, 96, 97, 101, 103, 104, 105, 108, 109, 112, 113, 114, 117, 118, 121, 122, 125, 128
Kuzume, Naoyuki, 85, 86, 90

Lae, 74
Las Pinas (Luzon), 111
Lavarak, John, 36
Leapfrogging Strategy (described), 75
Lear, Ben, 96
Leyte, 99, 100, 101, 102, 103, 108, 114, 122
*Life* Magazine, 63
Lingayen Gulf, 103, 104, 105
Luvaas, Jay, 7
Luzon, 34, 99, 100, 101, 102, 103, 104, 105, 106, 107, 108, 109, 110, 111, 112, 113, 114, 118, 121, 122, 125
Lyman, Charles, 80, 81

MacArthur, Douglas, ix, x, xi, 21, 22, 33, 34, 35, 36, 39, 40, 41, 43, 44, 45, 47, 48, 49, 50, 51, 54, 55, 56, 57, 58, 59, 60, 62, 63, 64, 65, 66, 67, 68, 69, 73, 74, 75, 76, 77, 81, 82, 83, 84, 85, 86, 87, 88, 91, 92, 93, 94, 96, 97, 98, 99, 100, 102, 103, 104, 105, 106, 107, 108, 112, 113, 114, 115, 117, 118, 119, 120, 121, 122, 124, 125, 126, 127, 128, 129
Madang, 75
Malay Peninsula, 33, 35, 36, 41, 45, 89, 90, 98, 100
Manila, 16, 34, 75, 103, 104, 105, 106, 107, 108, 109, 110, 111, 112, 113, 114, 126
Mapia Atoll, 99
March, Peyton, 10
Marianas Islands, 85
Marshall, George E., 24, 25, 26, 28, 29, 30, 37, 39, 49, 60, 66, 67, 68, 75, 80, 84, 96
Martin, Clarence, 37, 49, 52, 66, 122, 123
McKinley, James F., 20, 21, 23, 30
McNair, Lesley, 35
McNarney, Joseph, 18
Mindanao, 99, 114, 121, 122, 123, 124, 125
Mindoro, 102
Mokmer Drome, 85, 86, 89, 90
Montgomery, B., 93

Morotai, 102
Mott, John, 46, 49
Mountbatten, Lord Louis, 29

Napoleon, 43, 101
Nasugbu Beach, 107, 108, 109, 111, 112, 113, 114
Negros, 114, 117, 118, 119
New Britain, 98, 102
Nimitz, Chester, 75, 85, 86
Ninth Army, 3, 68, 91
Ninth Division, 30
Ninety-sixth Division, 100
Ninety-third Division, 107
Noemfoor, 84

Obregon, Alvura, 8, 9
Ohio State University, 1, 3
Overman, Lee, 7, 8
Owen Stanley Mountains (New Guinea), 40, 42

Palawan, 102, 114, 115, 116, 117, 118, 120
Palico River, 109
Panay, 114, 117, 118, 119
Papuan Peninsula, 34, 35, 51, 58, 59, 64, 67
Paranque (Luzon), 111, 112
Patton, George, 3, 23, 67, 91, 93, 126, 129
Percival, A. E., 33
Pershing, John, 9, 16, 22, 52
Phillipson, Irving, 24
Port Moresby, New Guinea, ix, 34, 35, 40, 41, 42, 44, 45, 47, 58, 65, 67
Puerto Princesa, 116

Rabaul, 74
Reckless Task Force, 77
Reeder, Russell, 39
Rockhampton (Australia), 36, 38, 62
Rogers, Gordon, 37, 49, 59
Rommel, Erwin, 35
Roosevelt, Franklin, 27, 34, 65
Rupertus, William, 18

Saidor, 73, 76, 85
Saipan, 85, 86, 87
Salamaua, 74
Samar, 99
Sanananda, 58, 59, 62, 63, 78, 88
Sanga Sanga, 116

# Index

Schoeffel, John, 6
Second Army, 96
Sentani Lake, 76
Seventh Division (Australian), 41, 42
Seventh Division (U.S.), 100
Seventy-seventh Division, 28, 29, 31, 103
Shoe, Robert, 95
Siberia, 32
Sibert, Franklin, 122
Simonds, George S., 21, 23
Simpson, William, 3, 68, 91
Singapore, 33
Sixth Army, 63, 71, 87, 88, 95, 100, 101, 102, 103, 104, 105, 106, 107, 112, 113, 114, 115, 118, 120, 121, 125
Sixth Army Group, 3, 91
Sixth Division, 105
Soule, Robert, 110
Stearns, C., 23
Stilwell, Joseph, 18
Stimson, Henry L., 29
Subic Bay, 106
Sulu Archipelago, 99, 114, 115, 118, 120, 125
Sutherland, Richard, ix, x, 33, 41, 42, 46, 47, 56, 57, 58, 125
Sverdrup, Jack, 63
Sweany, Kenneth, 87
Swift, Innis Palmer, 96
Swing, Joseph, 107, 108, 109, 110, 111

Tagaytay Ridge, 110, 111, 120
Tanahmerah Bay, 75, 77, 79, 81, 82
Tenth Corps, 100, 122, 124
Tenth Infantry Regiment, 3, 4, 10, 31, 122
Terauchi, Hisaichi, 100
Third Army, 3, 38, 91
Thirtieth Division, 29
Thirtieth Infantry Regiment, 24, 25, 28, 31
Thirty-eighth Division, 106
Thirty-first Division, 114, 122, 124
Thirty-second Division, 33, 37, 38, 39, 40, 41, 42, 44, 45, 46, 47, 48, 49, 53, 54, 55, 56, 57, 58, 69, 71; training deficiencies, 39–40, 73

Thirty-seventh Division, 105, 113
Training: I Corps, 69, 70, 71, 78; 8th Army, 99, 116; small-unit, 69, 80, 99, 122, 123; realism, 72, 73, 80, 82, 83; initiative, 71, 80, 82, 83, 99
Tsukada, Rikichi, 104
Twentieth Infantry Regiment, 9, 31
Twenty-fourth Corps, 100
Twenty-fourth Division, 69, 70, 71, 74, 76, 77, 79, 82, 95, 100, 114, 122, 123, 124
Twenty-second Infantry Regiment, 7, 8, 10, 31

Urbana Front, 49, 52

Victor Operations, 114, 115
Villa, Francisco (Pancho), 8, 9
Visayan Islands, 99, 102, 114, 120, 121, 125
Voorhees, Tracey S., 129

Wainwright, Jonathan, 34
Wakde-Sarmi (New Guinea), 76, 77, 82, 83, 84, 85
Wake Island, 33
Waldron, Albert, 51, 53, 57
Warnock, William, 1
Warren Front, 49, 52
Watson, Edwin, 27, 28
Weeks, John, 17
Weigley, Russell, 17
West Point, 1, 3, 5, 20, 26, 27, 28, 51, 52, 56, 63, 78, 79, 81, 91, 97, 107, 122
Wewak, 75, 76
Wilby, Francis, H., 26
Willoughby, Charles, ix, 41, 42, 43, 47, 57, 83, 85, 100, 103
Wilson, Woodrow, 11, 12, 13, 15
Woodruff, Roscoe, 122, 123
Wooten, George F., 54

Yamashita, Tomoyuki, 33, 34, 100, 103, 104, 105, 114, 125
Yokoyama, Shizuo, 104

Zamboanga, 102, 114, 115, 116, 117, 118, 120, 125